MW01611259

CREATING RELATIONAL CAPITAL

CREATING RELATIONAL CAPITAL

A CustomerCentric Selling® Approach

BY
JOHN HOLLAND
&
ED WALLACE

With a Foreword by Michael T. Bosworth
Bestselling Author of *Customer Centric Selling*
and *Solution Selling*

John Holland and Ed Wallace
jholland@customercentric.com
edwallace@relcapgroup.com

Printed in the United States of America
First Edition

ISBN 978-1-60461-132-8

Book Design by Kimberly Coleman
Illustrations by Jason Coleman

The caricatures throughout this book are not intended as actual depictions of the persons represented.

Dedication

From John Holland

To my wife Linda and our three children Lauren, Johnny, and Katie. The house is now too quiet, but we enjoy watching your journeys. To my partners in CustomerCentric Selling®, Frank, Gary and Mike, for having the courage to break away from what had once been a wonderful endeavor to create another.

From Ed Wallace

To Laurie, Brett and Grant for the great joy you share with me everyday and your continued support of my business efforts. Special thanks to my mother, Connie and sister Jennifer for your ongoing inspiration.

Table Of Contents

Acknowledgements

Our great friend Jim Mullen has served in many roles throughout each of our careers from customer to manager, peer to respected advisor.

Jim was ultimately the connection that helped bring this book and our sales training workshop series on relational capital together. We thank Jim for his confidence and support throughout the process.

Simply Complex

Foreword by Michael T. Bosworth

The demand on salespeople is simple, clear and measurable: meet or exceed quota. As with major league hitters, whose batting average can be figured to several decimal places, a salesperson's performance can be quickly calculated as the percentage of quota.

But, notions of how to achieve the desired sales results are all over the map. Non-salespeople often think all that's needed for sales success is "having a nice way with people." Organizations give the sales force tremendous latitude in how to achieve quota—which may be a kind way of saying that they provide minimal assessment, development or support to the sales function. The 80/20 rule in most companies bears this out.

Managers typically promote a range of admirable behaviors in their salespeople:

- Call high and stay high
- Avoid leading with product offerings
- Establish value in the minds of buyers
- Keep their pipelines full
- Forecast accurately
- Avoid competing and negotiating solely on price
- Establish strong relationships with buyers at all levels

While these all are certainly desirable, managers don't always give much practical guidance about how to do these things.

In fact, many charged with ensuring that salespeople achieve their goals are often ill-equipped to do their jobs. Sales managers are generally former sales professionals who did well and were promoted. Their sales success was largely the product of instinct and intuition and they have difficulty articulating how they did it much less how to explain it or teach it to others. After receiving product training, a territory, quota and the mandate to sell, they were somehow able to perform at high levels on a consistent basis. There was no plan, it just happened. While on quota, these people had no need to follow a repeatable process that would be teachable to the people who now report to them. Their selling careers were a series of successful adlibs. How often do top sales performers go from "hero to zero" their first year after being promoted to managers?

What's the outcome of this situation? Recent statistics from Sales Benchmark Index show that, on average, a mere 13% of an organization's salespeople generate 87% of its revenue, 25% of salespeople do not generate enough revenue to cover their expense to the company and 40% of salespeople lose their jobs every year. Clearly, salespeople could use a lot more help in getting prepared to succeed in their jobs—and organizations would see dramatic benefits if they gave them this help.

The main problem is that intuition and instinct cannot easily be taught. Making calls with direct reports has little value if managers can't describe the steps they are going to take during a call and review them afterwards.

The skill of building relationships, however, can be developed. Creating relationships is fundamental to success in sales and in business as a whole. Instinctively successful sales professionals are largely practicing the principles of outstanding relationship building, whether they know it or not.

Creating Relational Capital, then, presents a truly fresh take on the principles—the science and the art—of building successful business and sales relationships.

John Holland is an experienced collaborator. In the past, he worked with Frank Visgatis, Gary Walker and me in breaking down the steps that top performers take in selling. In *Creating Relational Capital*, John has collaborated with successful sales executive and author Ed Wallace to build a process for establishing better relationships not only with your buyers, but with other people in your company and your life. John and Ed take you through a range of steps—from the rational to the anecdotal, from the theoretical to the practical—in an engaging way that sales professionals and their managers will find extremely helpful.

We've all heard many times the expression, "This is a relationship business," and there's no question that this comment is true. However, if I were a CEO, I would live in constant fear that my company's revenues were in jeopardy because, if a competitor's salesperson could establish a better or higher level relationship with any of our customers, we would lose the account. I would want my sales managers to be on the lookout for anything that would help them and their people to build outstanding business relationships in which client companies viewed them not merely as salespeople but as respected advisors.

Creating Relational Capital addresses several things that other books on sales do not by:

- dealing head-on with the negative stereotypes that tend to keep salespeople in a subservient, even apologetic, role;

- providing real and entertaining examples of great relationship building in action, illustrating the principles being discussed;
- building its case clearly through a logical model showing the steps leading to superior relationships;
- giving readers the practical tools to avoid the negative sales stereotypes and become respected advisors to their customers.

Many salespeople spend huge amounts of time trying to be well-liked by their clients rather than focusing on creating relational capital with these clients.

Sellers need to work hard to overcome the pervasive negative stereotypes about sales relationships, they need to be viewed as sincere, honest, competent, helpful and worthy of respect. If this book has one effect on its readers, I hope it is that—given a choice between being liked or being respected by a decision maker—they would opt for the latter. Buyers seldom make important purchases from people they don't respect, no matter how much they might like them personally.

So, given what is at stake with building outstanding business relationships—at stake for individual sales professionals, for their careers and for the organizations that depend on them for prosperity and growth—I highly recommend a careful reading of the contents of this book. It's an important first step toward understanding how creating relational capital will become the power behind your sales career, your sales force and your company's future.

Are Buyers Stereotyping You?

The value of relational capital in the sales world can be plainly illustrated in the following diagram:

The ideal state, the desired relationship with a client, is the role of *respected advisor*.

This role is based on great reserves of credibility, integrity, and authenticity developed to the point where the buyer values your advice on issues and decisions **not** directly addressable by your offerings. It is the strategic high ground and it validates that you have built strong relational capital with the customer.

Most of us, of course, have to work hard to get up to this point, starting at the first or second level shown—where we function or see ourselves as a "salesperson" or "sales professional."

The major determining factor of where the buyer places the seller is the degree to which the seller has overcome the negative stereotype. A large part of that is whether they are perceived as subservient in the relationship.

If relational capital is your greatest asset in a business relationship, negative stereotypes are your greatest liability.

One primary purpose of this book then, is to help make you acutely aware of these pervasive sales-related stereotypes, how much you may be buying into them, and to help you internalize the concepts of relational capital so you can go about the business of becoming a respected advisor to as many of your clients as possible.

The Baggage of Negative Stereotyping

How many mothers dream of the day their son or daughter will become a salesperson? Pose that question to a group of people and most will start laughing. Strangely enough, salespeople also laugh at the premise. We are all buyers at times and feel the same way about pushy or inept sellers that we encounter.

Parents will dream of their children becoming doctors, lawyers, teachers, engineers, etc., but somehow sales is placed at the bottom rung of the career ladder. For this reason, sellers carry baggage that creates unique challenges for them when trying to establish personal relationships with buyers.

Stereotyping is generally unfair but it is a reality. People who aren't salespeople grossly underestimate the skills needed to succeed. Many doctors, lawyers, teachers and engineers would be incapable of successful careers in sales. How often have you heard people say that someone "has such a nice way with people—he ought to get into sales." The qualifications of top-performing sellers go far beyond having a nice way with people and are in short supply:

- Above-average intelligence

- Entrepreneurial spirit
- Decisiveness
- Strong written and verbal skills
- Competitive nature
- Tolerates risk of variable income tied to performance
- Handles rejection well
- Willingness to be directly accountable for performance

Despite these requirements, when most people are asked to share adjectives describing salespeople, they still come up with words like *pushy*, *dishonest*, and even *sleazy*.

If you don't agree that a pervasive negative stereotype of sellers exists, consider this situation: You walk into a retail store wanting to buy a new television. You haven't done any research and therefore aren't sure what is available and what your requirements are. A clerk approaches and dutifully asks: "May I help you?" Remarkably, most people respond: "No, I'm just looking"!

This makes no sense given these circumstances, until you realize buyers are leery of salespeople who have not shown they are different from the stereotype. The buyer is concerned that the salesperson will try to "oversell" them by inflating their needs trying to maximize the commission, instead of helping the buyer find a match for their requirements. Often this is an unfair assumption, but as the old adage says: "The buyer is always right." In other words, perception is reality.

Once people become aware of this negative stereotype of salespeople, they begin to wonder why it is so pervasive. Our belief is that the vast majority of salespeople are associated unfairly with the "used car salesman" stereotype. We think this happens because of people's past experience and outmoded perceptions. Consider telemarketers (prior to the "Do Not Call List"), people selling cars, insurance and timesharing.

Most everyone has been subjected at some point to a pushy seller, and that experience becomes the basis for stereotyping. In the U.S. legal system you are presumed innocent until proven guilty. Salespeople, however, seem to fall under Napoleonic Law, in which you are guilty until proven innocent. If the title on your business card is anything related to sales, you are presumed to be pushy, dishonest, or even sleazy until you prove yourself different (if you get the chance). Buyers may have worked with many professional salespeople who provided a positive buying experience, but they remember the few who fit the stereotype.

Interestingly, salespeople in Eastern European countries are held in high esteem. There, sales became a lucrative new profession after the fall of Communism in the 1990s. Many mothers in Eastern Europe do hope their children will have a career in sales. Without the cultural baggage that Americans have inherited—the snake-oil salesman, the flim-flam man—there is no negative stereotype.

At some level, corporations have also bought into the negative stereotype. If you are a doctor, lawyer, engineer or research scientist, that title will be on your business card. Sales, however, is different. Think of all the creative titles you find on business cards of sellers: Account Executive, Marketing Representative, Regional Manager, and Business Development Manager. When was the last time you've seen "Salesperson" used as the title on a business card? Are those euphemistic titles fooling unsuspecting buyers?

Part of the problem is that most everyone views selling as convincing, persuading, overcoming objections, etc. Selling is done **to** the buyer versus done **for** or **with** the buyer. Human nature is such that most people prefer to *buy* versus *being sold*. It is a matter of control. When someone is buying they set their budget, evaluate options, determine their needs and make the final decision. When being sold, there is someone attempting to influence their decision.

Buyers prefer to be asked questions versus being offered opinions. To attempt to change the dynamic between buyers and sellers, we'd like to offer the way the CustomerCentric Selling® methodology defines sales:

> Asking directed questions to help a buyer achieve a goal, solve a problem or satisfy a need.

If a salesperson embraces this definition, the hurdles to overcome the stereotype are greatly minimized.

First impressions are powerful. If in the first few minutes of meeting a buyer a seller's behavior is perceived to be "salesy", the stereotype rightfully or wrongfully will be applied and ultimately getting the sale becomes more difficult.

Because expectations are generally set low initially, you have an opportunity early in meeting prospects to have buyers conclude that you are *different*. When meeting or talking to a buyer for the first time, the initial few minutes are critical. Most salespeople have either been trained or have concluded that one of their first objectives is to get the buyer to like them.

Consider that for a moment. Have you ever *tried* to get someone to like you? It is a decision another person has to make. Trying to force things can be a recipe for disaster. If the first few minutes of the relationship go poorly, either that sales cycle is over or it will take several meetings to have the buyer change their opinion of you.

We'd like to suggest an alternate approach. In meeting a buyer for the first time would you get off to a better start if your objective is having the buyer conclude that you are sincere (avoid stereotypical behavior) and competent (perceived as someone who can provide expertise and value)? Stephen Covey says the combination of being perceived as sincere and competent results in having people feel that you are trustworthy. When you consider the common adjectives used to describe sellers, how would your chances of ultimately succeeding be enhanced if the buyer considered you to be trustworthy?

Behaviors That Reinforce "The Stereotype"

Depending upon your offering, sales cycles can be lengthy journeys. In starting a long boat cruise, struggling merely to get clear of the dock can be a real challenge in and of itself. So it is in those initial exchanges with buyers. We'd like to alert you to some common issues and behaviors—ones that tend to invite the negative stereotype:

> **Appearance** – Before any verbal communication takes place, buyers get an impression of sellers based upon appearance in a matter of seconds. Today's wide range of attire in business creates additional challenges to salespeople trying to align themselves with buyers. Sellers call on companies that dress formally, some that are business casual and others that have casual Fridays. This increases the chance to be out of alignment with buyers.

> **Greeting** – The first words spoken by a salesperson when meeting buyers are often something like: "Ms. Green, I'm Ken Filosi. Thanks very much for meeting with me today." This

greeting has the potential to lead to a subservient relationship with the buyer. First of all, the buyer likely will be on a first name basis (Ken) while the seller is on a more formal basis (Ms. Green). Though subtle, the second sentence undermines your power as it implies the buyer's time is more valuable than the seller's.

Chit chat versus get down to business? – Some buyers want to take some time to put the seller at ease and get to know one another before the business portion of the call. Others, however, are busy and want to get right to the point. If a seller guesses incorrectly, the first few minutes can be awkward. A buyer who wants to get right into the substance of the call will view a seller who wants to make small talk as a light-weight. A buyer wanting to have some small talk will view the seller who gets right down to business as aggressive and impatient.

Some people try to make broad assumptions based on perceived regional differences (New Yorkers get right to business; people in Nashville want to get to know you first). But, if you guess wrong you are off to a bad start.

Rapport – Some sales training teaches sellers to scan the office for pictures, trophies, etc., and use those as a basis for building rapport: "That's a beautiful trophy. How often do you golf/fish/play tennis?" There are several potential negative consequences of using this approach:

o It is possible that the majority of sellers calling on this buyer have opened their calls in this manner. By using the same opening, you run the risk of being stereotyped.

o A buyer might view this as an insincere way to relate to them.

o The buyer may be busy and not want to discuss matters such as golf/fishing/tennis.

o If you are not knowledgeable about the topic you bring up, it could quickly become obvious and cause the buyer to conclude that you are insincere.

Business card exchange – How often right after shaking hands do sellers initiate an exchange of business cards with buyers? An executive who has granted a thirty-minute time slot may well expect the salesperson to start the meeting in a more meaningful way to gain interest and attention, instead of focusing on a trivial business card exchange.

Cultural alignment – Buyers vary greatly in their volume and pace of speech. A fast talking buyer from New York can get frustrated with a slower talking salesperson from Charlotte. The converse is true as well. Differences in verbal pace can be distracting and make communication more difficult.

Hyperbole – How much credibility do buyers give the opinions of salespeople who haven't proven themselves different from the stereotype? Assume you are a buyer meeting a seller representing a company you have never heard of. In the first few minutes the seller states:

o We are the leader in our industry

o Our quality is unparalleled

o I can reduce your costs by more than 15%

o A major benefit of our offering is ease of use

o We offer superior customer service

o Last year we achieved revenues of almost $10,000,000

Most buyers know immediately these are opinions offered by

a salesperson trying to sell them something. Mention this scenario to several people you know and share the last opinion with them and then ask: "If you had to guess, what do you think was the actual revenue this company achieved?" You'll be amazed at how low some of the numbers will be. Opinions and hype offered by sellers early in a relationship will usually be discounted by the buyer and increase the chances of being perceived as a stereotypical salesperson.

Being subservient – We mentioned previously that sellers have a tendency to position themselves as being subordinate to buyers at all levels. Consider the fact that sellers meeting a buyer for the first time will often thank them for taking time to meet. As the relationship progresses, think how often, when buyers ask for something, invariably the answer is a resounding "Yes! No problem." Even if you are successful in a buying cycle, consider the disadvantage you have when trying to negotiate price or terms to a buyer who has gotten whatever they have asked for throughout the process.

Some sellers may also be overanxious to set up a subsequent meeting with the buyer, which reinforces the concept that a buyer's time may be more valuable than that of a seller.

All of the above issues, fairly or unfairly, contribute to the stereotyping of salespeople. They damage or defer your ability to create relational capital with your buyers and internal resources.

You're Not Just in Sales—You're in Business!

Another important perspective to help you combat the stereotypes is to start thinking of yourself as a *business person*, not just as a salesperson. This book is about developing outstanding *business* relationships, not just sales relationships. While a great deal of the focus is the buyer-seller relationship, the principles also apply to other personal and business relationships as well.

For example, salespeople are commonly stereotyped in a negative way by people *within their own organizations*. We suggest you be aware that fellow employees in accounting, manufacturing, customer service, support, marketing, etc. have had negative experiences in their own lives with salespeople. There may be instances where good relations with these internal resources can make the difference to you in meeting a particular deadline in the sales process or even getting a particular sale.

Having outstanding business relationships with internal staff will help them conclude that you are sincere and competent, and can be a real asset in your success.

Michael Bosworth mentioned relational capital in his Foreword and we have mentioned the term several times as well. So what is relational capital then? We define this term in detail and elaborate on this important concept later in the book, but for now, think of it this way:

> **Relational Capital is the value created by people in a business relationship.**

The ultimate objective of creating relational capital is to have buyers see you less as a salesperson and more as a respected advisor. Effective relational capital development creates outstanding business relationships that are an important component to achieving outstanding sales performance by becoming a respected advisor

advisor to your clients.

We believe when sellers behave like and are perceived as business people—rather than just as someone who wants to get a contract signed—they elevate their professional status in the relationship. We will develop what it means to be a business person in the sales process throughout this book.

Developing these types of relationships is both an art and a science. We will also take you through a combination of anecdotal, theoretical, and practical steps to help you overcome the stereotypes and find your own way to balance the science and art of relational capital, on your way to more successful sales and business results.

First, we'd like to do this in an extremely easy and enjoyable way—through true stories that illustrate a great deal of what we're talking about. Later, in Part II, we'll get back to explaining more about relational capital and specifically how to overcome the stereotypes that keep you from creating it.

We'll begin with Ed's stories, told from his own experience and in his voice, to share lessons he learned years ago about sales, business, relationships and life—from a remarkably successful taxi driver named Max.

PART I

Ed's Sales Lessons
From Max

CHAPTER ONE

The Little Extras

A number of years ago, my sales efforts required a significant amount of travel. I didn't like being away from my family any more than necessary, so I became king of the day trippers. It got so that I could actually visit Minneapolis or Iowa for a meeting and still make it home for a late dinner the same day. I would leave the house around 5 a.m. to drive to the Philadelphia airport and return home in time to see Brett, our first child, for a few precious minutes before tucking him safely into bed.

The night before one of these trips, our car developed an engine problem. I asked my wife Laurie to reserve a taxi to the airport and as usually the case when she got involved, remarkable events began to unfold.

The next morning at dawn I waited anxiously for the taxi to arrive, and the second the doorbell rang I ran to the door so the driver wouldn't ring a second time and wake our baby. When I opened the door, standing in front of me was a tall, lanky fellow with glasses and the sort of calm, kind face you might see in a classic Norman Rockwell painting. I was about to learn that this was not your average taxi driver. And by this, I don't mean to imply he was anything like the character "Jim" from the popular *Taxi* sitcom.

He greeted me courteously. I grabbed my briefcase, locked the door and began walking with him in the dark toward his parked taxi. I soon realized this was no ordinary Philadelphia taxi either. It was an old-style British taxi—30 or 40 years old—with stately, rounded exterior lines, running boards, and a large rear passenger compartment. Even at 5:00 a.m., I could tell it was spotless. Climbing into the back, I settled into a luxurious leather seat, stretched out my legs, and felt a deep sense of comfort and relief. We began to drive and I noticed there was no noise—no scratchy dispatcher's voice barking instructions, no jangling music on the radio. A cooler within reach provided a supply of fresh drinking water. It was amazing!

As we pulled away, the driver turned around to introduce himself.

"My name is Max," he said with a smile.

"Glad to meet you Max," I said, and meant it. "My name is Ed."

"Nice meeting you, Ed."

As we drove, he asked me a couple of questions about myself. Since, like some people, I'm pretty much my own favorite topic, I was happy to oblige. He was a terrific listener and I found myself sharing a good deal about my life. He showed no trace of ego; he was completely focused on me. It was just him, me and the car, with no distractions. He took special note when I told him about our new young son.

For the next couple of weeks, when I needed a ride to the airport, we requested Max as my driver but found he was booked solid even for a 5:00 AM ride! After three or four tries, we finally got on his calendar with a good week's advance notice. Once again, I waited at dawn for the doorbell to ring. But this time, to my surprise, he merely tapped quietly on the screen door. He said he remembered we had an infant and knew that mom and baby needed all the sleep they could get.

During the next several rides to the airport in Max's marvelous taxi, we talked almost entirely about me and my life. (By now, you may have noticed that I was no longer driving myself to the airport). He asked about my work, where I was traveling to, my ambitions, my family. I could hardly believe how at ease I felt opening up to him.

Finally, I decided to ask him some questions for a change. So, he told me a few things about himself and his business, his day-to-day schedule as a taxi driver. He explained how busy he was and how he wished there was more time in the day so he could accommodate everyone who needed his services. He felt genuinely sorry he was unable to take care of them all.

His clients could not be easily categorized; they were all kinds of people. Businessmen going to the airport and elderly people going shopping. Groups of ladies going to the city for a day at the art museum, lunch, and a nice tour of the historic district, which Max was only too happy to provide. He didn't care who he was serving. Social status did not matter to him at all. To him, everyone was the same; he made no judgments. He had an interesting sense of peace about him.

Finally, I had to ask, "So, Max, how did you develop such a long list of loyal customers?"

"Simple, Ed," he said holding his thumb and index finger about an inch apart, "It's the little extras!"

And what exactly were the 'little extras' that Max was talking about? Sure, it was great fun riding around in his taxi; it was the only one of its kind in the area and attracted a lot of attention. Still, this was only a small part of what made Max a success—and he was a success. If you paid close attention to this bespectacled sage behind the wheel, you could see that his entire business philosophy was based on the 'little extras' that make the difference in a business relationship.

Arriving on time. Courtesy and warmth. Impeccable upkeep of the vehicle. Providing a quiet atmosphere during the ride. The drinking water. The thoughtful interest in his customers' lives. The listening and the remembering. The gentle tap on the screen door at 5 in the morning.

On the simplest level, Max's job was to provide a ride from one place to another. Any driver could do that, and do it on time, safely and courteously. But, when you rode with Max, the quality of the relationship, the conversation—the whole experience—was so enjoyable, supportive, enlightening and pleasant that you just didn't want the trip to be over. By the time we arrived at the airport, I would have far preferred to stay in the taxi talking to Max and let the plane fly to Cleveland without me. He had mastered the art of taking his so-called simple business from a merely transactional level to the level of high-value personal relationships—creating a memorable experience between human beings.

Over the past twenty years or so, it seems as though the art of developing business relationships has gotten lost in the barrage of sophisticated graduate school theories and the resulting management fads that have grown out of these theories. As much as cell phones and Blackberries can help keep us connected, they often serve as an additional barrier to real, in-person communication. Technology has accelerated the dehumanization of business over the last several years in many ways. Individuals we used to think of as business partners we now refer to coldly as "accounts" or, worse yet, "revenue streams" that we "ping" over our electronic devices!

If we lose sight of the fact that a *real person* is on the other end of that call or e-mail, then we miss the opportunity to enrich our sales endeavors and our lives with the growth and learning that comes from true interaction with others. Many people have taken the notion of work-life balance to mean that you only need to focus on the relationships in the "life" or personal part of that equation— when, in fact, there is tremendous gain to be had from treating your business relationships with as much care.

Riding with Max off and on during those years opened my eyes to how poorly I was managing my own business relationships. Max was the greatest developer of business relationships that I have ever known. I learned more about selling and developing relationships by taking Max's taxi to the airport than I have ever learned from a course, a book or any other individual.

As we mentioned, this book is devoted to exploring what it means to have real quality in your business relationships and how you can use it to positively impact your sales success. In many ways, of course, doing this is its own reward, because quality relationships are satisfying, enriching, and they allow you to sleep well at night. Still, it's also undeniable that such relationships almost inevitably lead to rewards of the more ordinary sort - the kind that help you exceed quota, pay the mortgage and send the kids to college.

"It's the little extras!"

Lessons Learned

As sales professionals, it is helpful to understand that there is baggage that comes with the very title "Salesperson" itself. Therefore, it is vital to change that perception from the outset - that is to introduce yourself to the prospective client/buyer and establish a foundation for building a partnering approach to working together, and ultimately creating relational capital.

The salesperson's first job is to exhibit this to the buyer at a level that opens the door for further discussion. Just as Max demonstrated this with his timely arrivals, the impeccable upkeep of the vehicle, the drinking water, and his respectful questions, the salesperson can also demonstrate this to the buyer by:

1. Listening for the buyer's goals and aspirations
2. Sincerely and concisely communicating his/her organization's value and capabilities
3. Asking pertinent and relevant questions (at a high level early on in the process)
4. Communicating an approach or a "path forward" to future discussions that leaves the buyer with the understanding that this is going to be a collaborative process.

Remember, people like to *buy*…they just don't like *to be sold*. A sales professional understands this nuance and is able to navigate the process in a way that facilitates each interaction that takes place. Over time, this raises the salesperson from a "transactional" mode to a respected advisor level.

Ed's earliest interactions with Max caused him to want to continue to use Max's services and to develop the relationship further. The job at hand for the salesperson is exactly that, and executing it is as straightforward as keeping it simple by showing clear interest in the buyer's goals and aspirations while demonstrating real sincerity and competence.

CHAPTER TWO

Mr. DeMarcantonio's Tomatoes and Dr. Fred

Laurie and I at one time had a neighbor named Mr. DeMarcantonio, who was not very friendly. He kept pretty much to himself, tending his vegetable garden, which came up to the edge of our driveway. He was outside in that garden every day from spring through summer, wearing a red Phillies cap, digging, watering and generally occupying all of his time until fall. I had attempted, though somewhat half-heartedly, to hold conversations with him on several occasions, but I never got anything more than a strictly cordial "hello."

Early one morning, shortly after the sun was up, I walked out of my door to meet Max for one of my airport rides and there he was actually *talking with Mr. DeMarcantonio*, having just a grand old time discussing something with great animation. They were smiling, gesturing, laughing—and obviously enjoying each other's company. I stayed back a bit so I wouldn't interrupt them. I could now hear them talking about the tomato crop of all things and what a great year it was going to be for home-grown tomatoes.

After several minutes of this friendly banter, Max looked up, noticed me standing there, and said goodbye to Mr. DeMarcantonio.

"Max, what in the world were you guys talking about?" I said as we got into the taxi. "I've never been able to get two words out of him!" My frustration was only thinly disguised.

"Tomatoes, Ed." Max replied.

"Tomatoes! But, how do you even know him?"

"We started talking one morning about our vegetable gardens after he spotted me admiring his. One thing led to another and on my last trip to pick you up for the airport, I left him some of my tomatoes. Doesn't he have a great garden?"

"Yeah, I guess," I said intrigued by how Max had broken through his wall. "But, I always thought he was just old and wanted to keep to himself."

Max paused a moment.

"Do you really know him to be unapproachable, Ed?" he asked quizzically.

He had me on this one. I said I knew Mr. DeMarcantonio was certainly older than I was, but I had no real basis for saying he was unapproachable. I hadn't ever invested the time in him to be in a position to make that kind of judgment. I guess Max was saying, "Who are you to judge this man who is your neighbor, when you've never made much of an effort to have a genuine conversation with him?"

Somehow, Max had a way of asking questions that delivered his message without being judgmental.

"I hear you, Max," I said. "But, how do I connect with someone who just doesn't seem interested in connecting?"

"Ed, the chances are always pretty good there's common ground somewhere, if you look hard enough to find it."

Come to think of it, Max was all about common ground. You felt it in his taxi—he knew people wanted to feel comfortable, calm, refreshed, and specially treated on their way to wherever they were going, and he had created the perfect environment for this. He knew his customers wanted to talk about themselves, and he had the passion to be interested in and knowledgeable about virtually any topic they might bring up. By providing a friendly, relaxing atmosphere, and by making the effort to connect with what was important to his clients, Max had no trouble at all establishing credible, common ground, even in a vegetable garden.

* * * * *

Fast-forward

I've started my own business selling billing and claims services to physicians and struggling to leverage every ounce of sales skills that I have. At the time, I had no customers, few prospects, and no money. I had been making dozens of sales calls into doctors' offices leading with my products and services and typical sales techniques. This resulted in sales figures that wound up right where you might expect them to be—marginal at best.

Then, on one of my calls I visit a doctor's office in the basement of a row home in an economically challenged neighborhood. As I enter, I need to duck my head down some to avoid hitting it on the doorway overhead.

While spending a few minutes in the small, wood-paneled waiting room, I noticed several books about walking with the doctor's name on the cover of each one. This guy really seemed to believe in walking for your health and was not very shy about getting that message out to his patients. I was a runner so the thought of walking versus running was very interesting to me.

Eventually, the nurse escorts me to one of the examining rooms where I wait for the doctor. The doctor enters, does not look up, but asks, "What are your symptoms?"

I clear my throat and say that I'm not a patient but I'm here to see him about his accounts receivable.

He takes my card, glances at it and says, "Mr. Wallace, you have sixty seconds, and you have just used fifteen."

At this point all of the sales training you have goes out the window and instincts need to kick in. After what was likely the longest five-second pause of my life, I took a deep breath and replied, "Doctor I realize that you're very busy, but I can't possibly do justice to explaining my services in that amount of time. Could I ask you a question, though?"

"Shoot," he says.

"In your waiting area, I noticed that you've authored several books on walking. I'm a runner and would love to know why you believe walking is better."

I realize I'm already passed the sixty-second deadline, but what do I have to lose?

The doc's face brightens up.

"I'll tell you why walking is better," he says. "Do you ever notice the faces of people who are running?"

I responded, "They look contorted."

"Exactly! Now, how do the people walking look to you?" he asked.

I got the point. He not only answers my question, but he goes on for thirty minutes about why I should start walking and why he's so passionate about it. I learn that everyone calls him Dr. Fred.

Dr. Fred's office manager is doing her job and has by now tapped on the door three times, but the doc is on a roll and waves her away again. He talks some more about his latest book. Finally, he pauses, looks at me and says, "What were you here to see me about again?"

I explain that my services could possibly help him with his accounts receivable.

He says, "Make an appointment to see Jane, my office manager. And here, take this and start walking tomorrow!" and he hands me one of his books.

During the next few weeks in working with Jane, I discover that Dr. Fred has the largest Blue Cross practice in the entire area, despite his humble office environment, seeing close to ninety patients per day.

While I did gain a few customers with the other sales strategies mentioned earlier, my approach with Dr. Fred lead to him becoming one of my largest and most profitable accounts. A strong business relationship that lead to referrals and forecastable revenue every month.

If I had to attribute the sudden turnaround in that first conversation with Dr. Fred to something, I would attribute it to watching Max and Mr. DeMarcantonio talk about tomatoes. That day, Max helped me realize to always try to relate to people at a sincere, personal level, by making the effort to find the common ground.

Fortunately, in most cases you have more than the 60 seconds I had with Dr. Fred. But, are there people you've known for months or even years with whom you've never established common ground?

Finding common ground is an early opportunity to establish credibility and a satisfying aspect of developing outstanding business relationships.

Lessons Learned

In most complex sales situations, finding "common ground" that ultimately leads to the credibility and competence required for outstanding businesses relationships, needs to be established over time by "meeting the prospect where he or she is." This can take a good bit of discipline and can be quite challenging for the "B and C" salesperson as it entails developing a skill for listening. By suppressing the urge to offer solutions too early in the process, and exercising the patience to listen and learn as much as possible from the buyer, salespeople can set themselves apart.

Not only do you learn more so you become better equipped to help the buyer develop **their** solution, but you also demonstrate respect for the buyer as a person and a prospective client. Again, this doesn't happen in a single interaction, but rather across a number of interactions over time, until finally it becomes an important part of the ongoing relationship. Establishing common ground is the critical first step to enhance your opportunity for being viewed as a respected advisor – where your buyer seeks your input on many of her business decisions.

CHAPTER THREE

No Cutting in Line

On one of my morning rides with Max, I asked if he also picked up any clients at the airport after he dropped me off—in order to maximize his income, pardon the pun.

"Hey Max," I said, "Seems like a waste of time just driving down here with me and not driving back with a fare."

"Well, Ed," (Whenever Max said, 'Well, Ed,' I knew he was going to deliver some counsel.) "I have an opportunity to do that every time I drop my clients off here." Then his voice kind of trailed off. "I actually did it once when I was first getting started—dropped off a client, went right around to Arrivals and picked up the next person in line."

"Wow, that really must have been a profitable trip for you, Max," I said.

"Not really, Ed," he said, sounding more serious than I expected.

"Why?" I asked.

"Well, what time is your flight?" he asked. We had just entered the airport complex.

I said that I had another ninety minutes.

"Can you stay with me for a few more minutes? I want to show you something."

"Sure," I said, "Where are we headed?"

Max circled around to an outlying lot near the Arrivals section of the airport.

"Ed, do you see that parking lot, with all of the yellow taxi's lined up?"

"Sure. Man, there are a lot of taxis over there!"

"Yes, and you know what else, Ed? Some of them have been there for hours," he sighed.

"Wow," I said, "They need to find a way to avoid that line."

Max paused. He knew I was still not getting it. Then he tried again.

"Ed, most of those guys are immigrants who have no education, they come to this country, somehow find money to lease a taxi, work from dawn to midnight, never see their families, and spend a great deal of their time in that line. The unwritten rule is that if you want an arrival fare, you wait in that line."

"So," I said, "one day, without knowing all of this, you picked up a fare and cut some other guy out of a fare to the suburbs." I was finally catching on.

"Yes Ed, and to this day I regret it and I won't do it again."

"Oh come on Max, it was only one fare," I said, attempting to rationalize for him.

"Yes it was only one fare, but I didn't play by the rules. Who knows, maybe that next driver in line only picked up a short, local fare for all of the time he spent waiting—because I cut in line and took the larger suburban fare. Someday, I hope the airport will regulate the process better. But, whether they ever do or not, I need to do my best to abide by the unwritten rules, the ethics of my profession."

My experience with Max and the taxi line was very compelling. After reflecting on his integrity over cutting in line at the airport, I realized how private the quality of integrity can be. It's really something for people to say, "She has integrity," but even more powerful for us as individuals to live it without any acknowledgement. The airport taxi situation at that time was wide open for abuse without any accountability, yet Max lived his integrity in the face of no real consequences other than of course, his own requirement to sleep at night.

* * * * *

Here's an example of how this played out for me

While I was working at a technology company, I was asked to develop a sales channel program to work with key influencers in our market. Corporate America was in the middle of its Y2K anxiety, spending billions on enterprise-wide application software and consulting to make sure everything would work when the clock ticked to 12:00 AM on January 1, 2000.

Our company was doing well by partnering with the key software vendors in our industry. However, we discovered a gap in our strategy around the Big Six accounting firms. (As you probably know, today they are down to the Big Four due to consolidation and Arthur Andersen's troubles.) We learned that these firms often influenced their clients' software purchasing decisions, particularly in our area of specialty. We realized that though our company had a good reputation, our salespeople didn't have much personal connection to any of the Big Six partners and managers who worked closely with our prospects and customers.

I began thinking about how we could work with these key influencers since our CEO was very committed to partnering to help deliver everything our customers needed. Armed with nothing but his support and my own blind gumption, I set out to meet the key national partners at each firm.

Getting in the door for a meeting with each partner turned out to be surprisingly easy – these are not easy contacts to establish – and should have been my first clue that something was not right. After the initial niceties, each Big 6 partner immediately confronted me with, "Why would we work closely with you, since you compete with us?" In the first meeting or two, I was truly caught off-guard by their view of our company as a serious competitor. We had always viewed these firms as potential partners, and both a source of referrals for us and a place to refer our customers for consulting.

I realized we had a big integrity issue; apparently, they were still harboring bad feelings over our company's attempt several years earlier to get into consulting in their field of expertise. This was our own "cutting in line" issue. It took a lot of reassurance from our CEO and me to convince them that we were no longer interested in this area, and that it was worth their time to even pursue a more collaborative partnership.

It took many months of meetings, calls, and some key social time together to help these firms understand our true intentions, rebuild trust, and to prove to them that we were viable partners.

At last we were on a roll, working with each firm on the best way to partner with us, so their professionals would become expert and certified on our software—leading to potential consulting opportunities for them and positive buying decision influence for our company.

Life was great, until they started talking to Legal. Now, I have some great friends who are attorneys, so this is no slight to them, but even they would agree that legal departments can really slow down a process.

Apparently, what we were proposing amounted to partnerships and their whole structure and culture was based on *being* a partnership.

They didn't partner *with* anyone, rather they kept everything proprietary, and if they didn't possess a competency they either built it or went out and bought it.

Time to get creative.

I suggested to our CEO that since we had rebuilt trust, that we should use this renewed quality to everyone's benefit and do business with these firms on a simple handshake. No contracts, no formal agreements.

I explained that it could take years just to reach formal agreement on something as simple as an engagement letter. By that time, we would have missed the Y2K opportunity. I said we had pretty much defined the program, built it so each firm could have its own identity, and I felt my relationships with the partners were on solid ground. He said, "Why not?"

With another round of meetings to present our radical proposal (during which I had to pick a couple of Big Six partners up off the floor), I assured them that our CEO and I would personally stand behind this kind of arrangement putting our reputations in the industry on the line.

Miraculously, each firm agreed to our concept.

A parallel challenge you will face when developing business partnerships is working with your internal operational folks to make the partnership work. The last thing that well-oiled finance, customer service, sales, IT, and education groups need is for some business development or salesperson to approach them with a partnership such as this and disrupt their protocols, controls, and established routines.

We were fortunate in this case to have collaborated with each of these key groups throughout the process so when it came time to turn the switch on with the Big 6, everything went very smoothly. It did not hurt of course that outstanding business relationships were forged with these folks over the years resulting in support for such a challenging project.

After three years in the program, our company earned significant referral revenue annually and the Big Six consulting practices were each generating several times that amount in revenues from working with our products.

To top it off, we were even able to get them all to come together for an annual conference to collaborate on common issues — something previously unheard of in their fiercely competitive environment.

How did this happen?

Certainly, this accomplishment required a lot of one-on-one time talking with the national partners, and lots of time meeting with various Big Six practice offices. It took constant availability to help with questions and conflicts, and consistency of judgment when judgment calls were needed. And it required some political savvy to navigate the process, with each firm believing it was the best and competing with the others at every turn.

But behind all that, what really made it possible was our determination to build an environment of fairness, ethics, and trust. We wanted to create an atmosphere of integrity in these relationships where they could trust us as well as each other, and concentrate on the potential for expanding the size of the pie for all versus the usual concept of everyone fighting for the biggest piece of a limited pie.

In other words, even the big boys will do business on a handshake if they trust you not to cut in line.

Lessons Learned

This is a great lesson for salespeople, especially when their success depends on the long-term relationships that lead to repeatable product/service sales revenue. The buyers of these products and services are required to make many conscious decisions over long periods of time to choose those services over and over again. To ensure that the answer to each of those decision questions continues to be "yes," the salesperson should strive to establish impeccable integrity in the eyes of his client. Integrity is exhibited by certain characteristics in these interactions with client partners. Examples include saying "No, you won't need that" when appropriate, and by offering help for no fee at times.

Developing the relationship over time, taking the time to listen, understanding the client's overall situation, and offering solutions only in a way that meshes with all of the other client partner's business issues, demonstrates a truly consultative, integrity-based approach. You are then doing what is best for your client, doing it because it is the right thing to do, and that is practicing integrity at a level that would make Max proud. Remember, the simplest definition of integrity is, "doing the right thing when nobody is watching."

CHAPTER FOUR

The Power of "I Don't Know"

After many rides together, Max began to realize that I was taking a lot of the things he was saying pretty seriously. I was relatively young and impressionable, so one day Max turned to me and said, "Ed, you know I enjoy our conversations. But I hope you're making your own careful decisions on the matters we discuss, because I would feel awful if something didn't work out for you because you took some comment I made too seriously."

At that point I needed to come clean with Max and admit that I was seeing him, to some degree, as a surrogate father. He had such a fatherly, caring way; he listened to me and guided me. I confessed that my own father had passed away recently and that getting to know Max had gone a long way toward filling the hole that remained in my life.

"Max," I said, "I don't mean to put you on the spot, but your advice has been important to me."

"It's OK, Ed." he said. "Let's make a deal. From here on in, I'll keep that in mind and maybe I can be more of a mentor to you, since a mentor helps you find your own truth rather than imposing his truth on you. How's that work for you?"

Now, this was well before mentoring became a mainstream approach in the fields of leadership and management. I had hardly ever heard the term, except maybe in an old *Kung Fu TV* episode. Yet Max, my friendly taxi driver, was offering to serve as a mentor to me.

Next, Max had a revelation or two of his own to share with me in return. He said that I was filling a need for him as well.

"You know I enjoy my time with all my clients but when you and I get together the entire trip is different. You listen to what *I have to say*! You've become a kind of student of my life experiences and that means a lot. Plus, I enjoy your company."

Then he paused awhile and started to speak again. He told me that before he drove a taxi, he had been an executive for a large company, at one point accepting an important assignment to work in the Middle East in the late 1970s. Unfortunately, his assignment coincided with the Iran hostage crisis in 1979—in which 66 American diplomats and civilians were taken captive in the U.S. Embassy—a situation that dragged on for fourteen months, bedeviled the Carter administration and cast a long shadow over U.S. foreign affairs. It had been an extremely challenging and dangerous time to be an American working in the Middle East.

By that time Max had learned a variety of strategies for developing relationships and as well as the protocols for survival, communication, looking out for others in the community, and managing the day-to-day logistics of living and working under hostile conditions. He had to become an expert, not only in his original field of business, but in the cultural, political and economic realities that dominated every aspect of life there at that time.

But, at some point, once the crisis was resolved he came to a decision that he'd had enough—of the politics, the pressure, the danger, stress and anxiety. He thought hard and deeply about what was important in his life, and he began to reorganize his priorities. He moved his family back to the United States. He desired to live a simple life of service to people, taking the lessons he had learned about human nature, relationships and life, applying and sharing these freely in a helpful way. This was the point at which he purchased a taxi and set up his business providing rides, wisdom and friendship.

Through our relationship, Max told me he had found not only another client, not only pleasant conversation, but someone who understood his life work and to whom he could, in effect, authentically share it with, in the hopes it would continue to benefit others in some small way. Our relationship went beyond seller and client and had become a friendship.

Now I knew some experiences and events that shaped Max's approach to life that I hadn't known before, and Max learned some essential personal things about me that he hadn't known before. This put our relationship on a much more authentic basis. By being willing to "come clean" and simply be who we were at that time, we were better able to appreciate and help each other in ways that made a difference.

Being True to Yourself

This has been a key lesson for me in my life and business. Too often, we put a lot of energy into keeping up a façade in our business relationships—an appearance of strength, expertise, influence or success—for fear that others will see us as weak or vulnerable. To the contrary, I've found that when I'm comfortable just being who I am—to be authentically me, without embellishment or bragging—people tend to believe and respect me, and we make more progress in whatever project stands before us.

Often, the willingness to be your unvarnished self will result in the words, *I don't know*. I learned that a big turning point in a career is being able to admit this to yourself and others. No longer needing to "fake it until you make it" as the saying goes. To Max, these three words were like magic. He thought one of the hardest things for business people, especially as they are trying to move up the ladder, is to admit openly that they don't have all the answers. Saying *I don't know in a sales situation,* can open the doors to a healthy discussion about possible solutions and resources that could lead to an answer. The fact that the sales person may be admitting that he or she isn't the ultimate source of wisdom on the matter in question is not relevant; what *is* relevant is that everyone is able to focus on the need itself and how to meet it most effectively, together. Intellectual honesty is rare air these days.

On this point, I witnessed an amazing phenomenon in my son's fourth grade class during Observation Day. The teacher was going over some math problems, and they were challenging—at least to me. Yet, the kids were absolutely fearless in their attempts to answer each question. They had no anxiety over possible failure or what the others thought of them—only enthusiasm to attempt the challenge. They embraced Max's magic words, *I don't know*, and relished the task of finding the right answer.

We're often so guarded in our business relationships, so afraid to show our real selves. Think about all the meetings you've been in where an executive is droning on with a presentation—(Picture actor Ben Stein with his dry delivery in front of a meeting room)—and everyone in the room is just following the words on each slide, mentally glazing over and not willing to engage in any real discussion. I believe that it is because we're afraid of the dynamics, the politics of the people in the room, afraid of what they would think of us, or what might happen to our job if we said something that implied we didn't totally comprehend everything being presented.

I recall a story that Max shared about a very successful, retired CEO who launched a cottage industry out of her home and wound up being an industry giant. She was one of his regular riders and once shared with him an experience about a talk she was giving to a small group of former colleagues on a topic that she had basically built her reputation on. When asked what seemed to be a very fundamental question, she responded, "You know, I never thought of it that way!" The room went silent because everyone had a perspective on the topic yet the expert was freely admitting that she did not know. Guess what happened? Her former colleagues recognized and were comfortable responding to her authenticity. They made the issue a rallying point of common ground resulting in a spirit of "we'll work this out together". Committees were formed and a whole new strategy emerged that basically reinvented the previous work of the CEO. The corporation achieved significant growth again as a result of the strategy, people were promoted, and new jobs were created.

In the same way that "I don't know" can be a powerful phrase that reinforces authenticity in relationships that sellers have with buyers, there are also times when you do know that a particular offering is not right for a customer. Sellers that create relational capital are usually thinking long-term buyer satisfaction versus short term gains.

Lessons Learned

The kernel of wisdom that salespeople can take away from this chapter is a simple one, but difficult to execute. The key notion is that the salesperson is not the ultimate source of wisdom for addressing the client's every need, but rather a respected advisor who acts as a resource for the client partner. Think of the stress this takes off the salesperson if he/she can execute at this level. Your interactions go from trying to "sell" your product/service into a situation to working collaboratively with a partner to understand a situation and to explore ways to meet needs and enable buyers to achieve their goals or solve their problems. In such situations, sellers sometimes do not need to close because buyers will volunteer to buy!

The challenge for "B and C" salespeople is to learn to block out the pressures to meet quota, close business and keep the boss happy. Sometimes this can require you to tell a buyer not to buy a particular offering. One needs to "internalize" this concept, exercise the discipline to listen, and demonstrate to the client that your desire to help is authentic. This will lead to respected advisor status over time. This is a status that will serve you throughout your career and your life.

CHAPTER FIVE

Remember 168 and Bellybuttons

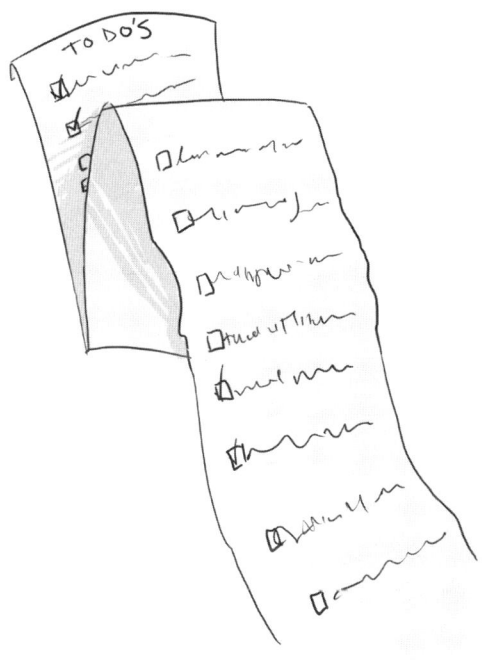

This chapter is about the importance of time. Max taught me a simple lesson about time which has a lot to do with making it possible to have outstanding business relationships. And his lesson is simple; but, I figured if I was distracted enough to need a simple lesson like this, you may be too.

On yet another trip to the airport, I was a bit detached and Max commented, "Seems like you're pretty busy today, Ed?"

"Oh, sorry Max, I've got proposals, memos, expense reports—and that's not the half of it. I just can't keep up!" I sighed.

"That's got to be very frustrating. Seems like you're caught in a vicious cycle," he said.

"Right, and that cycle seems endless. Any suggestions?"

Max knew he was on the spot again, but without changing his vocal inflection, he asked, "Do you know anything about the number 168, Ed?"

"168, 168? What's that all about?" I asked.

"Well, think about it," he said. "What could it represent?"

"Max, I'm drowning here, and you're playing paint by numbers with me! Can you give me a clue?" I asked frantically.

"Okay. We all have as much in common with the number 168 as we do with having a bellybutton." Max continued.

168 and belly buttons, now I'm really lost.

"Think Ed, think about *time* Ed. That's what you're asking about. Think!" he asked.

"Time is days, weeks, minutes, hours…." I mulled.

"Hours! Now you're getting warm," he cheered.

"Hours? There are 24 hours in a day and I don't have enough of them."

"OK, and how many hours are there in a week?"

Uh,…I am now multiplying 7 times 24 in my head and guess what? It comes out to 168!

"Max, you rascal, you could have just told me that right off the bat!" I responded.

"You know Ed, then it may have been too easy and you might not have recognized the value in knowing that number." He mused.

"I still don't see the value," I said. "We all have bellybuttons and we all have 168 hours in a week. So what?"

"Precisely, we all have the same amount of time. We also have a great deal of freedom in the ways that we choose to use it. Ed, how do you think the leaders of all the big corporations got to where they are? How did they find the time to do everything that had to be done to make a living, develop new skills, develop relationships, advance their careers and lead these global businesses?"

I proudly confessed, "*I don't know!*"

"Well Ed, I'll tell you," he started "they have the same amount of time in the day as you and me, but they make a choice on how to spend their time because it is what they want to do, what they believe in. I made a choice to drive a taxi, but in my own way because I wanted to spend my time in service to my clients, whom I also consider my friends. You know, if you like what you're doing, you'll never work another day in your life."

He continued, "You appear to have chosen to try to squeeze a lot of busy activity into your time. Ever wonder what that activity is producing?"

I could not say anything else at that moment because we arrived at the airport.

"What airline today, Ed?"

"USAir, thanks," I said.

With that, I had to leave Max's lesson on time, but I had a lot to reflect on during my flight.

* * * * *

Fast Forward

I took a corporate sales position with a major corporation. I had a pretty decent first year, but part way into the second year my boss stopped by my office one day and sat down. Now, Jim was not a hard-driving sales manager, more of a Father Flannigan counselor type. He asked how I thought things were going. This was his way of opening a conversation about how my performance was slipping, without saying, "Ed, your sales are off." And they were well behind quota.

I answered, "Jim, I keep working harder and harder, but my sales aren't improving. In fact they're getting worse."

"Seems like you need to think about where and how you're focusing your time, Ed," he said.

So, despite my dedication to developing strong personal relationships, friendships that would turn into business relationships, I wasn't paying enough attention to all the little factors that tended to eat away at my time, making it increasingly harder for me to bring those relationships to fruition.

Jim talked for another few minutes, but I kept visualizing the word TIME above his head and remembering Max's comments on time from a few years before. We agreed that I would come back to him with some thinking on this problem and that we'd work together on a plan to improve my performance.

I remembered how simple time seemed when Max discussed it. He had basically reduced it to the ridiculous with the number 168 and bellybuttons, and emphasis on our freedom to use time as we chose.

So, I thought about how sales people spend their time. We look for commonalities with the buyer. We try to differentiate ourselves from the competition. We all prospect, we all have a sales cycle, and we all have a contract to get signed. We all try to make a monthly quota.

Not much there, so I dug deeper on each step in the process. As far as I could see, every step was essential. So, I began looking for a different approach, some way to be different and more effective. I thought about this for weeks. Jim was getting a bit anxious since his boss was getting a bit anxious.

Finally, one night I woke up and said out loud, "That's it, that's it!" Now I knew how Keith Richard of The Rolling Stones must have felt when legend has it that he woke up one night and jotted down the opening chords to the all-time hit song, *Satisfaction*.

Laurie woke up and asked, somewhat bemused, "Now what are you conjuring up?"

"I think I cracked the code," I said.

"Cracked what code?" she asked in a tone that indicated "he's at it again!"

"Honey, please just go back to sleep, I need to go and write this down," I responded.

The words that I wrote down were simply *Timing and Process*.

The next day I looked at my prospect list and asked myself the same question about each one: "Will they buy from me on the 24th of the month instead of the 31st?" I thought through all of them and was able to answer *Yes* for about 50% percent of the list.

I realized that I had been caught up in the same cycle that my prospects were caught up in, likely reinforced by my competitors. They were being encouraged or pressured to make buying decisions at the same time that sales people had to close business. It made for a very busy time during that last week of every month. Inevitably, I had to give away value in the crunch and my customers weren't always completing all of their ordering on time either.

So, I sat down with Jim and asked if I could try a strategy that created an internal deadline for me by the 24th of every month rather than the end of the month. He blinked, since he had been at this for many years and had never heard of this one before. Eventually, he OK'd the plan, but just for one quarter and with two conditions (these are nice tips for sales people by the way):

First I had to create two Top Ten Lists of prospects. I think that Jim must have been watching too much David Letterman at the time. To make the first list, I needed to be able to do something for the prospect every day to move them through the sales cycle. If I could not, then they could not be on the first list. The second list was there to catch all of those that I could not work on every day. This seemed fair enough.

The second condition and this is the one that would ultimately make or break my success with this approach was to be authentic enough *to ask each prospect for their help.*

I asked Jim, "Why would I ask for help?"

To this day Jim's answer remains incredibly ironic to me since he never knew Max, but seemed to be coming from the same place.

"Asking for help infers respect and people who respect one another, help one another!" he commented.

Jim went on to explain that whether you are in a sales process or any business relationship, asking for help is a very powerful request. It will determine right then and there whether you have built a strong business relationship. Jim knew that this would not only help me qualify my prospects but, that in many cases human nature could work in my favor as well by seeking help from fellow human beings.

So, armed with Jim's advice and support, I set out to contact each prospect who was close to a buying decision and asked for their help with my idea of closing business earlier each month. Now, everyone was not ready to do this, but many more than the 50% that I expected agreed at least to explore trying to get their contracts signed sooner. This got the process in motion.

After a few months, I was rolling. My orders were coming in by the third week of every month, our production people had more time to get their end-of-month orders processed and customers were receiving their orders sooner. Now, I was able to be out doing what I enjoyed best, prospecting—*building relationships*—while my competitors were still trying to close business. I felt I was always a few days to a week ahead of the pack—a very sweet feeling, indeed.

And guess what? That year, my telesales rep and I had the number one producing territory leading to the Sales Team of the Year award.

Upon reflection, I can trace this success not only to my lesson on time and how best to use this natural resource, but the knowledge of the inherent desire in people to want to help each other.

Comedian/philosopher Steven Wright once said something like, "Everywhere is within walking distance, if you have the time!"

I felt like - *Everywhere was within walking distance because I made the time.*

Lessons Learned

Time is an important concept for salespeople to consider. I wonder how many salespeople attach a dollar value to their time (the way other "professionals" – lawyers, accountants, physicians – do). When thinking of time as it applies to salespeople, three words come to mind – focus, priorities, respect.

Focus – first of all, we need to understand that time is one variable that impacts us day to day, and that we can exercise some control over how we use our time. Consider how you are spending time; are you utilizing your time in a way that helps achieve your objectives or does time work against you?

Priorities – related to the comments above, it is important to do first things first, that is, understand what are the more important tasks we have to do in a given time period, and then actually do them in the appropriate priority order. For example, if you are a person who needs to make lists and write things down, by all means do it --just don't make THAT a priority that bogs you down!

Respect – your time does have value. And so does your client/partner's time. Very often salespeople see more value in their clients' time than in their own. Consider treating your time as being as precious as your buyer's. For example, when managing the sales process, make sure that the time allowed to complete tasks allows for both you and the client to deliver high quality results to each while you make progress toward your mutual objectives.

Time is one of the most valuable resources a salesperson has. Be authentic with yourself. Does the time you're spending on a given project/task have a real chance to pay off? Stop every so often and examine how you're using your time. Internalize the value of it. When a salesperson understands that his or her time is valuable, that the time they spend helping, advising and working with clients/partners is part of the value they bring, it elevates them again to that respected advisor level where relational capital thrives.

PART II

How To Create
Relational Capital

CHAPTER SIX

The Importance of
Relational Capital

Ed's taxi driver friend Max was a unique character, a remarkable human being, and a natural and intuitive respected advisor. He knew by instinct how to practice the principles of developing and maintaining outstanding relationships that resulted in customer satisfaction, loyalty and repeat business.

But, many of us need a little help to learn how to do all this effectively, and it's critical to get all the guidance we can on just how to create relationships that are lasting and rewarding.

So, now that we've seen a great real-life example of someone who embodies the art and science of building sales relationships, we're going to take a look—in Part II—at the principles that operate beneath the surface every time such a relationship occurs. As we do this, you will see how developing outstanding business relationships is the most powerful antidote to the problem of the negative sales stereotypes mentioned earlier in the book.

The next two chapters present the concept and theory of relational capital in greater detail, examining its real value and how it is created in business relationships. After that, we'll revisit the question of sales stereotypes and show how—armed with an understanding of relational capital—you can avoid and overcome these destructive stereotypes and move your business or career forward through relational capital development.

A Challenging Environment for Sales

Sales is a very demanding profession. Salespeople face incredible challenges in their work—a competitive marketplace, difficult prospects, quotas to meet, and a constantly changing business environment. Many customers are team-based, which presents new dynamics in the sales process. Still, the relationship with their

"Champion" needs to be outstanding. Also, salespeople must work effectively with their own teams to help facilitate the sales process internally and externally. Last, the Internet and pace of communications puts business leader buyers on call 24/7 with seemingly little time for anything but meeting the bottom line. This limits the availability of the buyer to the salesperson.

On that point, the Harvard Business Review recently noted that there are two main factors colliding with traditional management process and structure in the 21st Century business environment:

1. The movement toward more collaborative management structures and team-based processes;
2. The urgency of work due to the pace of technology.

As recently as a couple of decades ago, traditional management structure was still largely intact, with the familiar hallmarks of vertical, command-and-control decision making that proceeded slowly within departmental silos.

With the tsunami of technological change occurring in the 1980s and 1990s—including the process improvements inherent in enterprise-wide systems like SAP and Oracle, and tools like Lotus Notes—traditional management has been widely replaced by flattened, matrix-style organizations. These organizations are characterized by collaboration and virtual teaming with distributed leadership and, at times, lack of clarity on who is actually making the decisions.

The flow of work and decision-making, which once could be traced to a single, isolated individual or department, is now broadly influenced by large numbers of project participants. Their collective stake in project outcomes creates a relentless sense of urgency that ironically slows down completion of the tasks at hand.

The Fundamental Value of Relationships

This challenging environment leads to new, dynamic complications for salespeople, not the least of which is the question of whether the internal buying committee team is actually making the *buying decision* or just making *recommendations*. Your access to buying committee members and to the actual decision maker is highly dependent on the relational capital you create with the Champion, since this is what will protect you from being associated with the negative stereotypes about sales people.

We use the term "blind date" to explain the dynamic where a Champion is willing to give a salesperson unconditional access to people that the salesperson has not met. This validates that the salesperson has now reached respected advisor status. The Champion is completely comfortable to provide the introduction—just like when someone arranges a blind date for someone they know. Of course, the business phrase for this is a "referral."

With all of these challenging dynamics, at a sales level, the quality of business relationships has suffered significantly; they're often reduced to a series of short-term transactions between Blackberries instead of real interactions between people!

How many times have you emailed your prospect when a phone call would have been more appropriate and effective? Each time you do this, you have missed an opportunity to handle business personally because it was convenient to do it electronically. While email is an effective tool for keeping in touch, many times our intent can get distorted or misunderstood due to the absence of vocal inflection or tone in email communications.

We should never lose sight of the fact that two constants remain true through all of these 21st Century dynamics:

1. Business is still fundamentally driven by *people and relationships,* not by technology or to-do lists;
2. People still need human interaction and desire to have outstanding business relationships.

After all of his years riding with Max, Ed still struggled to define in business terms his friend's seemingly intangible wisdom for developing outstanding business relationships. As he did a little research, he learned some interesting facts:

- Over half the market value of Fortune 500 companies today is contributed by intangible assets;
- These intangible assets include intellectual property, brands, corporate reputation, employees, acquired goodwill and customer relationships;
- These intangible assets are also critical sources of income, referrals, repeat business, financial growth and competitive differentiation.

In fact, the intangible assets comprised of customer, employee and supplier relationships are sometimes referred to at the organizational level as relational capital. The relational capital of companies is so important that some investors will pay a large premium above book value to own shares of these companies.

The same perception of value can be applied to salespeople when calculating and growing their personal net worth in life and business.

- Your intangible assets include your knowledge and skills, educational background, reputation and your personal and professional relationships.

- Your intangible assets:
  - o Provide access to business and career opportunities that generate income
  - o Attract people and sales opportunities to you
  - o Generate referrals and repeat business
  - o Create a network of people that can offer help and resources to you
  - o Make your life and career more enjoyable

These intangible assets can be viewed as your *personal* relational capital. Therefore, throughout the rest of this book, we will use the term relational capital to describe the value and the power of investing in business relationships on which the success of any career or client partner relationship is ultimately based.

The Qualities of Relational Capital

Now, let's connect the idea of relational capital to three essential qualities that Max modeled which go into building outstanding business relationships— *credibility, integrity,* and *authenticity*.

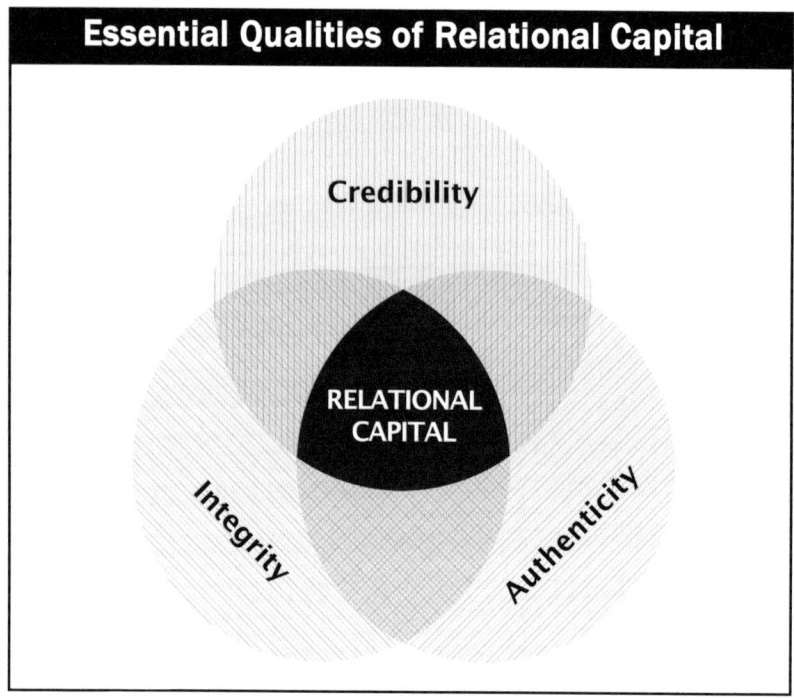

These are the essential qualities—the distinctive DNA that converges to create high levels of relational capital in business relationships.

Here's a more detailed explanation of these essential qualities:

Credibility

The American Heritage Dictionary defines credibility as "The quality, capability, or power to elicit belief."

The phrase "power to elicit belief" is compelling from a salesperson's standpoint because the buyer needs to believe in you and your competence to help them solve their problems as a critical first step before you can introduce anything for them to buy. This belief state may seem elusive, but will be a key differentiator in selling situations.

Everything about Max created credibility with Ed—his demeanor, enthusiasm, knowledge, and his taxi. Ed believed that Max was committed to being in service to his travel needs and that he was capable of delivering on that commitment.

Ed had zero credibility with Mr. DeMarcantonio because all Ed ever invested in the relationship was a "hello." However, when his opportunity came to develop credibility with Dr. Fred, instead of just pushing a sale, he took time to become personally interested in an unusual aspect of his expertise—walking and writing books about walking. His interest was sincere and consequently Dr. Fred believed that Ed was the kind of person with whom he would like to do business.

Integrity

Dictionary.com defines integrity as, "adherence to moral and ethical principles; soundness of moral character; honesty."

Salespeople hear all the time that they need to be honest and have integrity, yet how do they demonstrate such a private quality? Integrity is exhibited by certain behaviors when you interact with a client. Examples include saying "No, you won't need that from us" or offering to help for no fee, when appropriate.

Max's integrity was evident from the start of his relationship with Ed. Fairness, honesty and ethics were fundamental values to him, seen in how he treated his clients, charged for his services, how he sadly turned away business when he knew he couldn't deliver on additional commitments and how he refused to cut in line in front of his fellow cabbies.

In Ed's sales efforts with the Big Six, he first needed to overcome a perceived integrity issue before he could do business with them on a handshake.

Authenticity

The American Heritage Dictionary defines authenticity as "The quality or condition of being authentic, trustworthy, or genuine."

The key word is "genuine." This aspect of authenticity comes through when the salesperson begins to understand and demonstrate that she does not need to be the ultimate source of wisdom for solving the client's every need, but rather a respected advisor who acts as a trusted resource. Your interactions go from trying to "sell" your product/service to a situation of working collaboratively with a partner to understand a situation and explore ways to empower them to meet needs and solve problems. This approach allows buyers to **buy** versus being **sold**.

Ed's relationship with Max took on deeper dimensions after they became more authentic with each other, true to their own spirit and character and open about their backgrounds, circumstances and motivations. Ed learned a lesson about authenticity in being willing to tell clients *"I don't know"* and trusting that he would not lose anything in the process.

Despite the high-tech, fast-paced, constantly changing business environment in which all salespeople must operate, the fundamental and primary value of quality human relationships remains unchanged. While these relationships may seem to be an intangible or even "soft" kind of asset, in truth they are the key to avoiding the old, negative stereotypes that undermine business relationships. In other words, great relationships are the key to income-generating business and career opportunities, referrals, repeat business and to a full and enjoyable career.

So, now that you understand the basics of relational capital, the next chapter will explain the process involved in creating and *increasing* relational capital with your clients and all of your business associates.

Lessons Learned

A salesperson's focus on building outstanding business relationships is more critical today than ever before due to the move toward collaborative management structures, team-based purchasing processes and the pace and impact of technological change.

The essential qualities of establishing outstanding business relationships and relational capital are summarized in three words: credibility, integrity and authenticity. Exhibiting these in the context of the sales cycle helps you avoid the pitfalls of negative sales stereotypes and lays the groundwork for relationships which are long term, productive and profitable.

CHAPTER SEVEN

Relational Capital
Value Creation

Now that we've covered the basic ideas behind relational capital, we want to share with you our theory of how relational capital is created. Understanding this process will be essential to "Max"imizing your business relationships (pun intended) and reaping the terrific benefits that can result.

The following diagram depicts the Relational Capital Value Creation (RCVC) process that we will explore in this chapter:

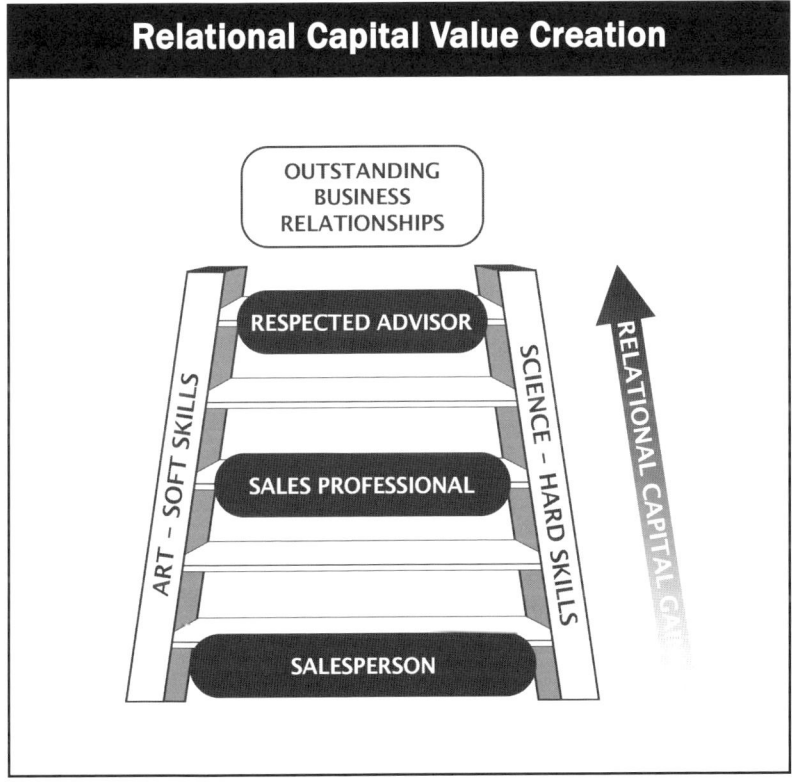

First, let's take a look at the process aspects of the model:

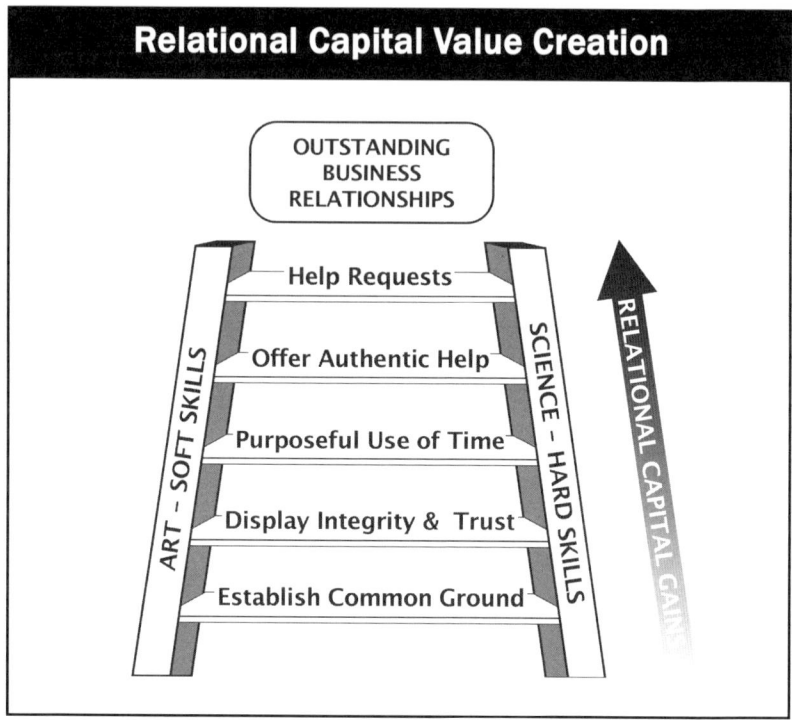

We mentioned that relational capital is created and developed through the combination of the qualities of credibility, integrity, and authenticity as well as the purposeful use of time that we learned about from Max. As a help in understanding this, think of the application of these qualities as your investment in a "relational capital account" with each of your clients or prospects. *Starting at the bottom of the diagram,* then, the sequence goes like this:

- **Rung 1:** Open relational capital accounts with others by *establishing common ground and credibility with them.*
- **Rung 2:** Secure and protect each account by displaying *integrity and trustworthiness.*

- **Rung 3:** Make investments in each account through the *purposeful use of time with clients*.
- **Rung 4:** Grow the value of each account by *offering authentic help and assistance*.
- **Rung 5:** Realize significant returns on relational capital through *asking for and receiving appropriate help* from clients.

Relational Capital Gains

Moving up the model, the qualities of relational capital—integrity, integrity, and authenticity—become stronger and begin to converge and culminate in an outstanding business relationship. This convergence occurs throughout the process and results in what we call *Relational Capital Gains* (represented by the arrow sloping up the side of the model)—a dynamic increase in reserves of trust and good will and the eventual attainment of respected advisor status. Relational capital gains lead to long-term, sustainable and ultimately outstanding business relationships.

Next, let's look at the frame of the process ladder and what we mean by hard and soft skills.

Hard Skills: *Science*

Think of the *science* component as the salesperson's ability to manage his or her pipeline metrics, product knowledge and technical competency. Our guess is that most salespeople can do this to a fairly effective degree. Consequently, the science component in sales has largely become commoditized in the minds of most buyers.

There is an old saying, "People do not care how much you know, until they know how much you care." So, a real differentiating skill in this area is the ability to select and adapt the parts of your technical competency and product knowledge that apply best to the specific buyer and situation.

Soft Skills: *Art*

On the opposite side of the ladder frame are the so-called "soft skills," or the *art* of the sales approach—the salesperson's interpersonal skills and behaviors, such as friendliness, approachability, good listening habits, follow-up communications, etc.

However, in defining the art of sales, most people use words like convincing, persuading, and overcoming objections. Buyers are viewed as people to be manipulated into buying decisions. Selling is something done **to**, not **for** or **with** buyers. While going beyond the scope of this book in terms of skills, one thing that can set you apart from other sellers is to change your view of selling.

Consider adopting the CustomerCentric Selling® methodology definition for selling offered in the Introduction of this book:

> Asking directed questions to help a buyer achieve a goal, solve a problem or satisfy a need.

Asking versus telling accomplishes several things. It involves buyers in the process and allows them to exert some control over the conversation. By asking questions, sellers know where buyers stand. Ultimately it supports one of Ben Franklin's quotes: "People are best convinced by reasons they themselves understand."

Asking also empowers buyers. With other things being relatively equal, empowering people to achieve their goals, solve their problems or satisfy their needs by using your offering can serve as your competitive advantage.

Balancing the Science and Art of Sales

Developing outstanding business relationships involves a careful balancing of the art and science of selling. Neither of these two components should greatly outweigh the other. Think, for example, about the effect of a salesperson entertaining clients to extremes or never talking about business, or on the other hand, always talking about technical specifications but never really listening to the client or relaxing enough to get to know the client on a more personal level.

The RCVC process provides a very effective way to achieve a balance between the science and art of selling. The stronger the relational capital gains, the easier it is to compensate for imbalances in the science or art of the sales process, which, in turn, contributes to improved performance and reinforces the quality of the relationship.

Creating relational capital gains in business and sales adds critical value in several important ways:

- High-value relationships are better equipped to weather inevitable business downturns and other uncontrollable factors;
- Relational capital transforms a business environment from a focus on transactions and tactical accomplishments to a focus on the value each party brings to the relationship;
- Relational capital helps people transcend the sense of urgency and panic that permeates much of today's work world, because both parties are able to operate on a

higher plane, working as partners that are better able to identify real issues and priorities and achieve real productivity for each other.

While being at a level of respected advisor with every buyer can be your goal, it is unlikely that it can be achieved. There will be contacts with whom you enjoy respected advisor status and others with whom you will need to work harder to increase the level of relational capital. Keep in mind that you have some level of relational capital with everyone you do business with. Given the impact that relationships can have on your sales performance, consider striving to upgrade each relationship regardless of how each person views your role.

Relational Capital Checklist

The first step in improving your relationships is establishing a base line of where you stand today. It may be difficult to accurately make these assessments, so we wanted to provide guidelines that can serve as indicators for you. We suggest you try to determine how you are viewed by some of your buyers as well as people within your own organization. Once you establish a base line, consider putting a plan in place to increase your relational capital with each person.

Relational Capital Checklist

The more of these you can identify as being present in your business relationships, the more likely it is that you are realizing the benefits of relational capital:

- ☐ You are able to view negative input from your customers as an opportunity to strengthen the relationship

- ☐ People from all levels in your organization take you into their confidence and seek your help and input

- ☐ You ask for help and receive it from colleagues

- ☐ Open and honest conversations with your manager do not put your career at risk

- ☐ You continue to be a valued reference for people as they move through their own career opportunities

- ☐ Your customer is confident that their buying decision (even if your price is higher) is the right one due to your relational capital with them

- ☐ Buyers are willing to recommend on a regular basis that their peers at other companies talk with you

- ☐ You are comfortable referring business that you cannot provide to others

- ☐ You ask for help and receive it from customers

- ☐ Buyers may ask your opinion about a candidate they are interviewing or a person they are considering for a promotion

- ☐ Customers share confidences with you and invite you into their planning processes

- ☐ Buyers solicit your advice on issues and decisions not directly addressable by your offerings

How do we learn to get it?

So, now that we have defined and analyzed relational capital how do we learn to get it like Max got it? How do we get to a place where we recognize the value of relational capital—where we focus on the people in the business relationship and their long-term objectives, not just the immediate, tangible products to be generated by the next transaction? How do we break through the new business environment processes and methodologies to get to real outstanding business relationships?

One way is to go back to basics and really focus on the essential qualities of relational capital: credibility, integrity, and authenticity. Since most of us already possess these qualities to some degree, how do we learn to appreciate them, value them and put them to more active use?

One answer is by "re-appreciating" these qualities that constitute outstanding business relationships and by remembering that most real accomplishments—whether it's the sale of a product or service or the advancement of a career—involve human beings listening to, understanding and helping one another in the ways that look a lot like a partnerships.

Without intending to do so, Charles Schultz, creator of the famous *Peanuts* characters, once gave an accurate description of relational capital by saying—"While people may or may not long remember who won what award, contest or prize or set which world record— they will always remember someone who has listened to them, appreciated or helped them in solving a problem or overcoming an obstacle."

The next chapter will expand on the model we just explained, but at a more hands-on level. We'll start by revisiting more closely the matter of overcoming negative sales stereotypes. With a basic understanding of what relational capital is and how to build it, you will be equipped to replace old habits and stereotyped attitudes and behaviors with substantive and productive relationships in which you reach respected advisor status.

Lessons Learned

Relational Capital Value Creation keeps sales professionals in balance as they move through the relationship development process. Relational capital is created and developed through the convergence of the qualities of credibility, integrity, and authenticity, along with the purposeful use of time.

These qualities can be thought of as the equivalent of basic investment principles. As a result, relational capital gains can be achieved by the following steps:

- Open relational capital accounts with others by establishing **common ground and credibility** with them;
- Secure and protect each "account" by demonstrating **integrity and trustworthiness**;
- Make investments in each account through the **purposeful use of time** with people;
- Grow the value of each account by **offering authentic help** and assistance;
- Realize returns **by asking for and receiving help** from clients.

Developing outstanding business relationships is a multi-dimensional process that evolves as the essential qualities grow stronger and converge in a business relationship to generate relational capital gains.

CHAPTER EIGHT

Overcoming Sales
Stereotypes

In Part One, you read about Ed's unique experiences and lessons learned from his friend Max the taxi driver—illustrating the essence of creating natural relational capital. In the first chapters of Part Two, you have just read about our theory of what relational capital really is, how it operates and how it is created in business relationships.

But no book on successful sales can be effective without giving the reader a practical, how-to guide, showing a way to apply the truths and theories covered in the book. That is what this chapter is for and we'll do this by looking in more detail at the five levels of our model leading up to relational capital gains and respected advisor status with your clients.

Overcoming Stereotypes

In the world of sales, much of the work to be done has to do with the overcoming of obstacles. In our view, the biggest obstacle to successful sales is the prevalence of stereotyped notions of what a salesperson is and does. These are the images in the prospect's mind that prevent that individual from seeing the salesperson as a sales professional or respected advisor. These same limiting images also exist in the minds of salespeople themselves and in the view of others within their own organizations. These stereotypes were the subject of the Introduction to this book and every chapter up to this point has been presented with the purpose of informing you of the power of relational capital in replacing such stereotypes with long-term, substantial and rewarding interactions with your colleagues, associates and clients.

So, in this chapter, we want to start by revisiting the stereotypes covered in the Introduction and look closely at how to go about overcoming them throughout the RCVC. Keep in mind that this process of overcoming these negatives will take place first in our own minds, but will have an effect on our behavior and, ultimately, on the way that clients and associates see and relate to us.

By now, you may have realized that you exhibit some of the stereotypical behaviors mentioned in the Introduction. That certainly doesn't mean you aren't successful in sales, but we hope you agree that avoiding those behaviors at the outset when trying to establish new buyer relationships can provide a definite competitive edge.

So, let's drive deeper into the RCVC process and create a "how to" road map to help you first avoid having buyers apply negative seller stereotypes to you and then to create relational capital gains throughout the relationship.

Rung 1: Establish Common Ground

The first step in the RCVC process is opening an account (starting off the relationship) with the buyer. This task becomes much easier if you start the relationship by establishing common ground which demonstrates your credibility and competence over time.

The following common behaviors or stereotypical "traps" listed in the Introduction can now be converted into strengths using the first step in the process:

> **Appearance** – It is especially important to be in alignment with the buyer for your initial meeting. Attempt to dress at a level equal to the buyers you call on. If in doubt, err on the side of over dressing because it is easy to remove a jacket and roll up your sleeves if encountering a buyer dressed less formally than you. The matter of body piercing and tattoos are up to you, but consider what you really have to gain by showing these, versus the downside if the client would have a negative

reaction.

Greeting – When meeting a buyer for the first time, we suggest being the first to extend your hand while making eye contact and say: "Rob Sherman with the ABC Company. I appreciate the opportunity to meet with you today." The chances are the prospect will respond with "Kay Green. Nice to meet you."

A few things happen when using this introduction. First, most people respond with their first and last name, so it is now Rob talking with Kay rather than Ms. Green. Second, "appreciating the opportunity to meet," positions you as a peer with the buyer. It is appropriate at the end of a meeting to thank a person for their time, but isn't it strange to thank a person for their time **before** they've given it to you?

Chit-chat or get down to business? – After saying "I appreciate the opportunity to meet with you today," we suggest the seller remain quiet for 3-4 seconds. This allows the buyer to indicate which way they want to go. They will either initiate some small talk or may say something like: "I hate to rush you, Rob, but I've got a staff meeting in a half hour. Can you tell me why you wanted to meet with me today?" Pausing with a few seconds of silence allows buyers to choose where they want to take the conversation. Instead of trying to "light up the room," sellers that use this approach allow the host (most calls are at the buyer's location) to break the ice. If after 3-4 seconds the buyer has not broken the ice, assume the buyer wants to get right down to why you wanted to meet, and proceed with the business discussion.

Rapport – By using the last approach, you will most likely minimize situations where you guess wrong as to which direction the buyer wants to go. In the event that they initiate small talk, please be aware of how much time is spent (remember everyone has 168 hours in a week, even buyers!). After what you feel has been a reasonable period of time, you can say: "I've got a busy day and it looks as though you do as well. Can I tell you why I wanted to meet with you today?"

This approach minimizes the chances that you will have learned a great deal about the buyer personally, but spent little or no time understanding if the buyer may have some need for your offerings.

Business card exchange – In granting a 30-minute appointment, most buyers would hope there is some potentially compelling reason you are making a call. An early exchange of business cards does little or nothing to build momentum in a call. As with the 3-4 seconds of silence, we suggest that you let the buyer initiate an exchange of business cards. You will likely find buyers don't do so very often. If you feel an exchange of business cards is appropriate and the buyer hasn't initiated it, make the request at the end of the meeting.

Cultural alignment – Studies show that sellers that can align with a buyer's verbal patterns achieve greater alignment and more effective communication. Volume is readily modulated so consider trying to match the volume of your buyer's voice. Pace can be an issue. Most people can slow down in an attempt to match another's pace. The problem emerges when a seller from one part of the country speaks 80 words per minute calling on a buyer from another part who speaks 160 words per minute. In these cases, we suggest that the seller try to reduce the number of words they speak and avoid spinning lengthy yarns. Balancing things out will put you in better alignment.

Hyperbole – Buyers have become accustomed to the reality that salespeople have a tendency to embellish and overstate the strengths of their company and the offerings they sell. One psychologist says that during the first 15 minutes of establishing a relationship, nothing but absolute truths should be stated in order to gain credibility and trust.

In first calls with prospects, sellers are often guilty of trying to tell buyers how they should feel about their company and offerings. One suggestion is to consider the conclusions you would like the buyer to arrive at and then offer only facts that would help the buyer draw the same conclusion. Here are some examples:

Stability – ABC was founded in 1987 and has no debt.
Innovation – Last year ABC invested 8% of gross revenues in R&D.
Customer loyalty – ABC enjoys a 95% customer retention rate.

Salespeople that offer facts to allow buyers to draw their own conclusions stand out from their competition. It is much easier for a customer to hear that last year your company achieved $9.8 MM in revenue versus being told that last year ABC achieved revenues of "almost $10 MM."

Being subservient – The goal is to establish a peer-to-peer relationship. One way of accomplishing that is to utilize the concept of *quid pro quo,* which amounts to giving and getting in return. Let's say a prospect says: "Rob, I'm interested in having you provide a lease quotation on the networking hardware we will be installing." Most sellers would enthusiastically say "Sure thing."

An alternative response can be even more effective in positioning yourself as a peer: "I'd be happy to provide a quote, but can you first provide an Annual Report and a banking reference so I can determine the rate we can extend?" Two positive things result. First, the buyer understands that this relationship will be a two way (give-get) street. Second, it will quickly disqualify buyers who aren't really interested.

We believe a seller brings expertise and resources that enable buyers to improve business results. The buyer has the ability to decide to spend money with the seller. This can be the foundation of establishing a peer-to-peer relationship. When asked to do or provide something (i.e. a demonstration for a non-decision maker), it is reasonable to ask for something in return when appropriate (access to the decision maker if the demonstration meets the buyer's expectations).

Another way to treat buyers as peers, in terms of the relative value of your time, is to set an expectation early in the call. State something to the effect that by the end of the meeting both parties should be able to agree if further meetings or discussions are appropriate. This can help put the buyer at ease and helps establish that each party's time is valuable and to be respected.

We cannot over emphasize how important Establishing Common Ground is as a salesperson's critical first step in developing the buyer's view of you as credible and competent and building a mutually agreed path forward. Remember you are still stereotyped as a salesperson at this point in the process. The objective during the first few minutes of a call is that the buyer will conclude you are different than his or her stereotype of a seller.

Rung 2: Display Integrity and Trust

Having avoided or prevented negative sales stereotypes and having gained the respect of the buyer and set the foundation for relational capital, you now can begin to generate initial relational capital gains in order to "secure the account" with buyers by Displaying Integrity and Trust.

The simple definition mentioned earlier that summarizes the concept of integrity is, "doing the right thing when nobody is watching." This definition can be expanded to include doing the right thing when the buyer is unaware of something the seller knows.

In fact, doing the absolute right thing may go contrary to the short-term goals of either a salesperson or their company. If your buyer perceives you as an advocate, he or she will draw positive conclusions about your integrity. Don't forget:

- Max's lesson—*no cutting in line;*
- Ed was able to get Big Six accounting firms to do business on a handshake because they trusted him and his company to do the right thing.

Max and Ed demonstrated integrity in their relationships and then validated it—"paid it off"—by living up to whatever commitments they made during the process. That is the point when integrity changes from being a private quality to being an outward or public manifestation of trust. We've heard one technology business owner express it as follows: "Your integrity only comes through publicly when you make commitments and then deliver on them." His favorite mantra is, "Commitments are promises, and promises kept help you make a trusted partner."

It might be helpful for you to reflect upon times when you had opportunities to display integrity with your buyers and how you reacted. Sales can be a pressure cooker where numbers always need to be made, but you will often find that sacrificing short-term gains can pave the way for long-term rewards—like being able to sleep well at night.

Rung 3: Purposeful Use of Time

Buyers used to have more time to spend with salespeople. Not that long ago, it was more common for salespeople to take buyers to lunch or dinner and to entertain them in a variety of ways. But, the economy slowed in the early 1980s and big layoffs resulted, dramatically increasing the workload of those who were able to retain their positions. This trend—creating a lean and mean, results-focused environment—has continued in different forms and rippled throughout the economy ever since. This has caused a dramatic change in the "schmoozing" or the Art aspects of selling.

Now, buyers may meet sellers over lunch because there isn't any other time to meet. Instead of relaxing with a cocktail or glass of wine, Diet Coke or ice tea have become beverages of choice. Executives who once had staff answering their phones now use voicemail and manage it themselves. Today's executive is adept at using Word and writing his or her own letters due to the constant pressure to improve the bottom line.

In the past, sellers would "stop by" to talk with customers and "face time" with buyers was viewed as a valuable part of customer relations. Today's environment is different. In the same way sellers have belly buttons and only 168 hours in a week, so do buyers. Everyone is under pressure to be more productive. Phone calls, teleconferencing and webinars have reduced the number of face-to-face calls. In many respects, business relationships have largely become depersonalized.

Even in this environment, some sales managers still focus on the *number* of calls their salespeople make, with little regard for the *quality* of the calls, nor the *value* the call has for the buyer.

So, to help promote the more purposeful use of precious sales time, we have developed a simple planning tool which has proven effective in almost any situation.

The Relational Capital Outcome Planner

This tool can help optimize your time, your team's time, and your buyer's—supporting increased relational capital gains throughout the process. First, let's look at the components of the Relational Capital Outcome Planner (RCOP):

Relational Capital Outcome Planner

Purpose: A Purpose Statement is the cornerstone of the RCOP. The purpose statement is broken into three parts:

We are doing this task:

TO *(describe the specific work to be completed)*

IN A WAY THAT *(describe the benefits of the work to the individual or group charged with the task)*

SO THAT *(describe the benefits to the larger organization to which the individual or group is connected).*

Outcome: Itemize the specific, tangible results of the work

Process: List the steps you will follow to achieve the Purpose and Outcome

Remember that a process is a series of activities, the output of which is a value to the customer or your company. When completing the Process section you should be sure to check and re-check the Purpose and Outcome to be sure that the process you're setting up addresses all of the elements contained in each.

On the next page is a very simple example of using the RCOP in a sales scenario:

Illustration of the
Relational Capital Outcome Planner

Scenario:

Linda needs to organize a meeting with the buyer and her internal team. The buyer needs to get answers from Linda's subject matter experts on particular aspects of the product. Linda will use the RCOP to facilitate the meeting.

Purpose:

> **TO** create a dialogue between the buyer and our R&D team
>
> **IN A WAY THAT**
> - o Establishes our company's credibility with the buyer
> - o Begins creating relational capital with key players from each team
> - o Provides insights to the buyer
>
> **SO THAT** our buyer can confidently continue with a favorable evaluation of our company

Outcome:

1. Closure on buyer's questions
2. Relational capital gains development for both organizations
3. Agreed to next steps

Process:

1. Upfront agreement on expected meeting outcomes
2. Brief introduction of team members and their backgrounds
3. Dialogue and answers to buyer's open questions, responsibility for closure on open items
4. Document agreements and next steps

The Relational Capital Outcome Planner allows you to stop and plan out effective interactions with your prospects and support team. This planning will ultimately translate into more productive meetings, a favorable view of your company as you move through the sales cycle, and relational capital gains for you, from your buyer and your internal team—because you made the most effective use of their time.

Valuing Your Own Time

Salespeople understand the value of their client's time. Sales professionals and respected advisors go a step further in valuing their own time. Have you ever thought about the value of **your** own time?

Here's a simple formula to determine the value of your time:

Calculating a Salesperson's Hourly Worth Example

Annual Compensation:

Base salary	$ 60,000
Benefits (40% of base)	24,000
Commission at quota	90,000
Total compensation at quota	**$ 174,000**

Some people would merely stop here and convert the total compensation to an hourly rate. However, companies expect a return on the money paid. The true value of a seller's time to a company must include the benefit derived from them achieving their quota. If we assume a seller achieves exactly her quota, this added calculation produces a more accurate number:

Annual Contribution to Company Profits

($1,500,000 revenue) x (20% margin) =
$300,000 bottom line contribution

So, adding the seller's total compensation to her annual contribution made to company profits, results in the Total Worth of a Seller's Time.

Total Worth of a Seller's Time

Total compensation at quota	$ 174,000
Annual contribution to profit	300,000
Total Worth	**$ 474,000**

The calculations to get to an hourly cost are now easily completed:

($474,000/year) / (12 months/year x 160 hours/month) =
$246.88/hour

In summary, the Total Worth of a Seller's Time is the cost of her total compensation at quota plus the net profit from sales generated. In this example, it equates to about $247/hour or $474,000 per year to the company!

We mentioned in Chapter Five that time is one of the most precious resources a salesperson has. Stop every so often and examine how you're using your time. Internalize the value of it, and then as you relate it to the time you spend helping, advising, and working through the buyer's issues, you will transform your relationship to the respected advisor level where relational capital thrives.

Rungs 4 and 5: Authenticity—Offering and Asking for Help

Once you have worked to establish common ground with your buyer, have demonstrated your integrity and trustworthiness and have shown your respect for and productive use of other people's time, you will be approaching the level where you achieve status as a respected advisor. At this point, you have accumulated relational capital gains and are in a position to interact with the buyer in very authentic ways. Often, opportunities to do this come in the form of questions from the buyer on issues that go beyond the realm of your offerings as a seller.

These requests start with phrases like:

- "What do you think of …….?
- "What is your opinion of …..?
- "We're looking to fill (a position). Can you recommend anyone?"
- "I'm thinking about promoting Lauren. How do you think she'd do in that position?"
- "Can you help us with?"

These types of inquiries indicate that the buyer now views you as a respected advisor and resource.

At this stage, you not only have a tremendous advantage over sellers calling on this buyer who have not achieved this status, but you can begin to generate significant returns from the account. You have transcended merely providing an offering and pricing and have become a business partner. As your relational capital gains increase in intensity, the questions you are asked stray farther from the scope of areas addressable by your offerings alone.

A word of caution: while it's flattering to be asked these types of questions, please don't forget the power of saying "I don't know" or saying that you don't feel you are the best person to provide guidance on this matter. Trying to provide advice in areas where you lack expertise will ultimately deplete your relational capital.

Now that you have provided authentic help in response to their question, the relationship becomes a two-way street at the top of the Relational Capital Value Creation process. The buyer can and will continue to ask you for different kinds of help. But, you have also earned the right to ask for the buyer's help at this point.

We all know that unsolicited advice is often unwelcome and unappreciated. On the other hand, unsolicited *requests for advice* usually have the opposite effect. It is flattering to the person who is asked and it gives them the opportunity to try to help somebody they respect.

As with most things in life, moderation is the key. Sellers should limit such requests to issues that matter and are worthy of their buyer's time.

As we mentioned in Chapter Five, Ed's sales manager knew that Ed had built enough relational capital gains with his buyers and recommended that now was the time to ask for help to kick start his sales numbers. This was the first and likely last time that Ed would need to make this request and the results were outstanding.

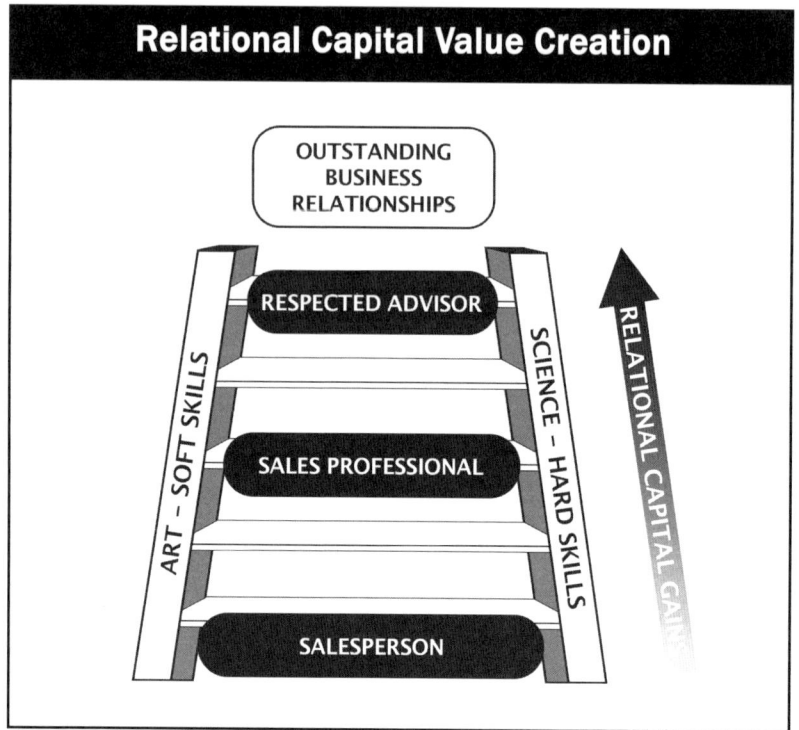

Lessons Learned

So, here you are, at the top of the ladder. You've created relational capital gains through conscientious attention and new skill development based on the requirements of the process. You've addressed and headed off negative stereotypes of salespeople, in your own thinking and in others'; you've shown integrity, valued your time and others' and achieved a level of authenticity that elevates you from the run-of-the-mill image of salespeople and positions you as a respected advisor in the hearts and minds of your customers. And, in doing all of this, you've kept the science of your sales techniques in balance with the art—the human interaction skills of listening, empathy and communication.

We've shared a great deal on the subject of relational capital. But, of course, there's more. We would feel negligent if we didn't leave you on a strong note of encouragement and support. How better to do that than to return one last time to Max?

CHAPTER NINE

Max's Legacy —
Your Opportunity

Max didn't go around telling people they should move away to learn a few life lessons. He simply wanted to share—in his unique, subtle, way—how he valued and appreciated the basic, good things in life, and his sense of how people should treat one another and conduct their business.

The journeys that Ed took with Max were full of deep insights because, in the normal course of a largely commoditized business, he added incredible value and became a truly respected advisor.

Any one of these lessons would have been a substantial legacy for most people. The ideas are so simple, so basic—is it really so hard to "turn down" our electronic devices just as Max turned down the radio in the taxi, allow ourselves to listen to each other, find the common ground, to be honest and ethical, and to be genuinely ourselves, with no artifice? Max sure didn't think so.

Most importantly, at the end of the day, all of "the little extras" that Max loved to talk about and modeled during the course of his business, all the subtleties resulted in the following real indicators of success:

- **Customer loyalty** – A rider needed two to three weeks notice to get a ride with Max. In fact, most riders scheduled their next ride as they left the taxi, so Max need only look to his calendar to understand his forecast.

- **Increased revenue per ride** – While the cost of the fare did not change, Ed tipped Max more than he would other riders and it is likely that others did as well.

- **More frequent trips** – Ed opted for the taxi ride more often than driving or taking the train to the airport; this equates strongly to the power and benefits of repeat business from existing customers.

- **No competition** – Max basically became "competitor proof," Ed and most other riders only used alternative drivers when Max was not available.

- **Respected Advisor** – Max became Ed's respected advisor by not only providing an outstanding trip and pleasant conversation every time but much needed wisdom and guidance on business and life – well beyond the scope of Ed's expectations.

Max called this phenomenon 'the little extras'. Fifteen years later, we're calling it 'creating relational capital.' Either way, we believe that how people know and regard you is the most important element in any business relationship's path to success and to your own personal success.

Michael Bosworth spoke in the Foreword about the "simply complex" mission of a salesperson. He equates this mission to that of a major league batter's performance and how readily measurable it is yet how difficult hitting for a high average can be.

Along with the hard metrics of batting for a high average and exceeding quota, baseball and building outstanding business relationships can also be very subtle. Think about how players need to get a lead of a certain length to steal a base that keeps an inning going, eventually leading to a game-winning run. This subtlety pays off in the long run for the winning team.

So too, can the subtle aspects of building outstanding business relationships payoff for salespeople. Many of the experiences and steps we shared in this book to develop outstanding business relationships involve subtle planning and execution rather than event-like proclamations – leading to how people know and regard you.

Our friend, Paul Jones, another VP of Sales, once asked, "Why don't all salespeople act like Max?"

Before we could, he answered his own question, "It's because building relationships is hard work that you need to think about every day!"

It is hard work that needs to be practiced every day, but in the end, sales professionals and respected advisors who can create relational capital benefit in the same way that Max did. Customers try to give them every opportunity for additional business. The few times buyers have to go elsewhere, they are apologetic.

Respected advisors serve buyers that are far less price sensitive than ones that are perceived as being "salespeople." While needing to be competitive, buyers understand the value the seller can provide and that the lowest price is not necessarily the best decision. One of our buyers had a plaque on the wall of his office that said: "The bitterness of poor quality lingers long after the sweetness of a lower price."

We guess Max was right on target when he said,

"Whether at work or in your taxi—it's the little extras that make all the difference."

* * * * *

Now that you understand how to get to the top of the ladder, try the Respected Advisor Exercise to evaluate your relationships and develop plans to improve them.

Respected Advisor Exercise

Think of three different buyers—one who views you as a sales-person, one where he/she views you as a sales professional and one where he/she views you as a respected advisor:

1. _____

2. _____

3. _____

Now, using the respected advisor relationship as your reference point, ask yourself why the other two relationships are not at the same level:

_____

_____

_____

_____

_____

Identify the steps you would take to move these two relationships to the next level. In other words, how would you interact with these clients to deepen and strengthen the relationship and move your role toward that of respected advisor:

_____

_____

_____

_____

_____

_____

_____

_____

APPENDIX

SUGGESTED READING TO HELP YOU ON YOUR WAY TO BECOMING A RESPECTED ADVISOR

Here's our short list of recommended additional reading. We hope that you can find time to enjoy at least a couple of these if you're looking for further, thoughtful analysis and truly creative thinking on subjects that complement what we've been espousing.

Customer Centric Selling, by Michael T. Bosworth and John R. Holland – published by McGraw-Hill, 2004

Great insights on how to avoid the sales stereotype and become a true buying facilitator.

Swim with the Sharks Without Being Eaten Alive, by Harvey McKay – latest edition re-published by HarperBusiness Essentials, 2005.

This is a great book written by a real business guy!

Selling the Invisible, by Harry Beckwith – Warner Books Inc, 1997.

Beckwith shares a great deal about the importance of business relationships beyond any marketing work that we have found.

The Seven Habits of Highly Effective People, by Stephen R. Covey – A Fireside Book, published by Simon and Schuster

Written in 1989, this book is as powerful today as it was almost twenty years ago. An "evergreen" classic for all time.

Everything I Need to Know I Learned in Kindergarten, by Robert Fulghum, published by Villard Books, a division of Random House, 1986

Max would certainly agree!

NOTES

CustomerCentric Selling® is a registered trademark of Customer Centric Systems, LLC

BlackBerry is a trademark of Research in Motion

The Max stories and Relational Capital theories are adapted from the book *Fares to Friends: How to Develop Outstanding Business Relationships* by Ed Wallace, copyright 2006

Relational Capital Value Creation is a servicemark of The Relational Capital Group

Microsoft is a registered trademark of Microsoft Corporation

Oracle is a registered trademark of Oracle Corporation

SAP is a registered trademark of SAP Corporation

Harvard Business Review *"Wild West of Coaching"*, 2005

David Reibstein, PhD *"Connecting Marketing Metrics to Financial Consequences"*, November 17, 2004

ABOUT THE AUTHOR

John Holland
Co-Founder
CustomerCentric Selling®

In coauthoring and helping launch CustomerCentric Selling® in 2002, John Holland leveraged more than 20 years' experience in sales, sales management and consulting. As a sales consultant, he helped many diverse organizations design and implement a standard sales process. He has worked with technology, overnight delivery, language localization, leasing, temporary housing and financial services companies.

In 2003 McGraw-Hill published *Customer Centric Selling* which John and Mike Bosworth, the original author of *Solution Selling*, co-authored. Holland has had articles published by Sales and Marketing Executive Report, Selling Power and American Salesman. He was commissioned to write a white paper on best practices in CRM focusing on integrating automation with sales process. He has spoken on various topics for organizations including SMEI, The American Marketing Association and Software Success.

Holland earned a degree in Mechanical Engineering from Northeastern University before starting his career in high technology with IBM's General Systems Division. In addition to being one of four principals in CustomerCentric Selling®, John serves in an Advisory Board capacity with selected companies, providing guidance and advice about product direction, service offerings, and overall sales and marketing strategies.

John Holland can be reached at www.customercentricsystems.com or jholland@customercentric.com.

ABOUT THE AUTHOR

Ed Wallace

President and Founder
The Relational Capital Group

Throughout his 25 year career, Ed Wallace has served in various sales and executive leadership roles. At Vertex, Inc., Ed participated in key sales and leadership roles as the company grew from $1 million to over $100 million in revenue. As VP of Business Development, he oversaw a number of strategic partnerships and acquisitions, including Arthur Andersen's Tax Technology Enterprises unit.

During this time, Ed learned a great deal about the value of outstanding business relationships and developed his philosophy of Relational Capital – the value created by people in a business relationship. This philosophy is manifested in his book – *Fares to Friends: How to Develop Outstanding Business Relationships.*

Seeking new challenges, Ed has launched The Relational Capital Group to help sales professionals understand how to build outstanding, high performing business relationships through Relational Capital development workshops and executive coaching.

Ed frequently speaks to corporations and groups, leads workshops on the value of Relational Capital development and has appeared on a variety of radio and television programs.

Ed was a Teaching Fellow at Drexel University while he earned his MBA, has a B.S. in Accounting (cum laude) from Villanova University, and has a CPA designation in the State of Pennsylvania.

Ed Wallace can be reached at www.relationalcapitalgroup.com or edwallace@relcapgroup.com.